The
Floating
Battlefield

To my father,
who, many years ago, managed, after much time and effort,
to persuade me that the study of business and finance could
be both interesting and worthwhile. Thanks, Dad.

The
Floating
Battlefield

Corporate Strategies in the Currency Wars

Gregory J. Millman

American Management Association

Library of Congress Cataloging-in-Publication Data

Millman, Gregory J.
    The floating battlefield : corporate strategies in the currency
wars / Gregory J. Millman.
        p.   cm.
    ISBN 0-8144-5987-0
        1. Foreign exchange administration—Case studies. 2. Risk
    management—Case studies. 3. Business enterprises—Finance—Case
    studies. I. Title.
HG3851.M54   1990   89-77449
658.1'55—dc20   CIP

Printing number

10   9   8   7   6   5   4   3   2   1

Contents

Acknowledgments

I would first like to express my gratitude to all of the corporate executives whose cooperation made this book possible. Many people participated in taped, on-the-record interviews that provided the foundation for each corporate case history related in this book; I owe a special debt of thanks to those corporate executives who took time to arrange lengthy discussions of the principles and practice of currency risk management at their own companies, patiently fielded my many follow-up questions, and helped with the process of fact checking, even to the point of reviewing the initial draft to ensure technical accuracy.

Therefore, I would like to extend such recognition as an author may by publicly acknowledging my debt to John Clerico, Vice-President and Treasurer of Union Carbide Corporation; to Frederick W. Zuckerman, Vice-President and Treasurer, and Hank Spellman, Assistant Treasurer, of Chrysler Corporation; to Stephen Hendrix, Vice-President and Assistant Treasurer, and James Johnson, Foreign Exchange Director, of SmithKline Beckman; to P. C. von der Porten, Treasurer of Finning Ltd.; to Paul Milbury, Assistant Treasurer, and Thomas Downing, Manager of Foreign Exchange, at Digital Equipment Corporation; and to David Guthrie, Manager of Worldwide Corporate Foreign Exchange Risk for Monsanto Corporation, Jim Hirschfield, Manager of International Administration for Monsanto Agricultural Company, and David O'Neal, Manager of Financial Analysis for Monsanto Chemical Company.

Professor Donald R. Lessard of the Massachusetts Institute of Technology, Alfred P. Sloan School of Management, was kind enough to spare time from a busy teaching, research, and consulting schedule in order to share his views and perspective on the developing science of currency risk management—a science to which his own contribution is immeasurably great. I appreciate both his generosity and his patience. Consultants Robert Baldoni of Eurocurrency Management Corp. and Abe George of Multinational Computer Models, Inc., spent long hours discussing their respective approaches to currency risk and helped me to appreciate the "why" behind the variety of ways that risk may be defined, discovered, and dealt with.

Among the bankers who assisted with technical information about financial instruments and their application to corporate strategic currency risk management, Jeffrey Barr, Vice-President with Citicorp, and C. William Schroth, Managing Director of First Boston Corporation, deserve particular thanks.

I especially thank Howard McLean of the Currency Options Institute in Philadelphia, John Powers of *Intermarket Magazine*, and William Falloon of *Corporate Risk Management Magazine*, each of whom went far beyond the bounds of duty and even the expectations of friendship in their patient, detailed, concise, pointed reviews of the original manuscript.

Thanks to all of those whose names must go unmentioned but who provided valuable background information on currency risk management in their companies. I regret that they were not able to take public credit for the help they provided, but I am no less grateful for their assistance.

Finally, I want to thank Adrienne Hickey, Myles Thompson, Kate Pferdner, and Liz Murphy of AMACOM for their editorial assistance, early support, and sustained enthusiasm for this project.

Foreword

A measure of the extent to which companies really think about the impact of foreign exchange can be seen by calling up a database of companies that have registered filings with the U.S. Securities and Exchange Commission. Key in the words *foreign exchange* and run a cross-check against the listings; you'll discover that fewer than 10 percent of the 12,000 companies listed show any reference to the term in their SEC reports.

Why so few? First, bear in mind that companies reporting to the SEC tend to be larger, longer-established, and more sophisticated. They have access to expensive consultants, in-house economic staffs in some cases, and are big believers in planning. If they are multinational companies, they invariably study and compare the relative advantages for profits in wage levels, inflation, borrowing costs in different currencies, political risks, and taxation changes, among other variables. Yet for many, a variable such as foreign exchange is taken far less seriously than these others.

Fortunately, companies are now much more aware of the implications of foreign exchange than they were just a few years ago, and this awareness is growing. In the corporate ranks, American managers are coming of age, having only textbook references to stable foreign exchange rates. The real world has been anything but stable. Americans saw the U.S. dollar's value plummet and soar dramatically in several cycles over the past twenty years. The reactions were varied. Some decided to batten down the hatches, ride out the storm, and wait for calm to return. They locked in or locked out the impact of currency fluctuations. The parallel strategy in the accounting industry was to smooth out the earnings volatility on financial statements. But locking out currency volatility only works as long as the currency moves against you; when it moves in your favor, you suffer an opportunity loss that your competitors stand to gain. And using accounting to protect earnings from currency volatility is hiding from the real world. Although accounting can protect and smooth out earnings in relation to past performance, it doesn't protect future earnings from the hidden menace of eroding market share. When it comes to share of markets and profits, the smoothness of your earnings doesn't matter. What matters is keeping your currency-related costs below your competitor's.

Of course, it may be harder for American businesspeople to come to grips with the impact of foreign currency fluctuations than for others elsewhere. The United States is a continentalwide supermarket, bigger than the collections of markets of countries in Europe or Asia-Pacific. For the most part, it exports to itself while it imports from the rest of the world. It operates on one currency, one monetary policy, one set of commercial laws, and possesses a highly efficient system of internal transportation and communication. Competition is tough enough at home; foreign competition and foreign exchange do not come readily to mind.

They do in Europe and in Japan and in Australia and anywhere the domestic market is not big enough to be the sole support of a business. Thinking in terms of a foreign currency is just an extension of thinking in terms of a foreign language, foreign laws, and foreign ways of doing business. A foreign currency is an alternative valuation of money. Like those who can speak in one or more foreign languages, those who can think in terms of alternative valuations possess advantages over those limited to thinking only in terms of their own currency.

Unfortunately, thinking only in terms of their own currency is the way most people still think of foreign exchange. It is therefore implicitly regarded as something inferior to their own home currency. As a result, such people can become dangerously blind to the many more subtle business developments that lurk beneath the surface.

How's that? Consider how some U.S. multinationals might

have better weathered the 1981–1982 recession if they had known in advance how their foreign competitors would use a weak currency advantage to make inroads into their U.S. domestic markets. What if these companies had acted positively, rather than attempting to obtain the government's help in revaluing certain foreign currencies upward against the dollar?

Hindsight does not usually help those who have missed opportunities when acting decisively at a critical time could have meant a world of difference later on. In today's world, technology vastly speeds up the reaction time to even the most minute changes in market stimuli. The volatility of foreign exchange and other financial markets can benefit those who have the desire to put them to work. The principles of the foreign exchange market can be understood. The application of this understanding and the tactics selected are unique in each case. That is because they are strongly influenced by the traits of each company, such as the corporate ethos, the risk-taking penchant of management, and the unity of management and employees.

Because humans desire permanence and stability in all things, the seeming chaos and irrationality that mark the behavior of foreign exchange markets seem better off being reduced and eliminated to the greatest degree.

But neither the volatility nor its impact is likely to disappear. As world trade and global finance grow, so too does the volume of foreign exchange. Since the market is essentially unregulated in price movement, there are no real rules. What rules there are are being written by those companies that are dealing with foreign exchange in an ongoing, rational manner.

Some of those companies appear in this book, which details certain of their experiences, reactions, and strategies. Depending on your level of expertise, you may be impressed or dismayed by what you read. In either case, it is safe to assume that you will have learned something about yourself and your company's ability to react to foreign exchange—and how it can help you or ruin you.

JOHN G. POWERS
Founder, *Intermarket* Magazine

PART I

Understanding Risk

CHAPTER 1

Why Currency Risk Affects Everyone

The chaotic and volatile movement of currencies has serious implications for all businesses. Many managers have ignored currency
risk. But managers who ignore currency risk are rapidly disappear-
ing. From the silicon chip factories of Kyushu to the steel mills in
the valley of the Ruhr, from the tractor plants set among the
cornfields by Peoria to the frozen logging roads of British Columbia,
there is currency risk everywhere that money changes hands. In this
era of floating exchange rates, no business in the industrial world
may consider itself completely insulated from currency risk. For if
business is a war without bullets, then that war is increasingly
fought on a floating battlefield. Imagine an army that struggles
mightily to take a hill only to find that the hill, overnight, has
turned into a valley, and the plain onto which the enemy had been

3

beaten is now the high ground. Currency is such a battleground. Every company may be such an army.

Money, the measure of a company's performance, has no fixed value. A yen, mark, pound, dollar: Each currency is merely a function of the others, but the relative weight of each constituent currency keeps changing, so the sum is unstable. When currency exchange rates shift, the value of a company's assets, earnings, and costs shifts too.

This is not merely an accounting issue. The successful drive by foreign manufacturers to capture market share in almost every country means that now, even companies that never sell or buy abroad can be wiped out by currency moves. If a dollar is defined in terms of yen, then whether a dollar is worth 200, 180, or 130 yen can be an important fact for any business that pays out dollars or earns dollars. Except in those rare industries that do not include Japanese companies among the competitors, the yen-dollar relationship can well determine costs, revenues, profits, and market share for all industy participants. The same may be said of the mark-dollar, pound-yen, or franc-mark relationship.

In fact, changes in any currency relationship may determine the relative competitive position of companies that do not even buy or sell in any currency but their own. If the mark-yen exchange rate changes, especially if the change is substantial and sustained, there will be a change in the relative competitive position of German and Japanese manufacturers. A British company that competes with both German and Japanese manufacturers in the domestic British market faces a different set of competitive circumstances when the mark-yen exchange rate changes. If the currency shift has bestowed an advantage upon the German manufacturer at the expense of the Japanese, then the British company must adjust market forecasts accordingly. New questions must be asked: Is this shift a short-term anomaly, or part of a long-term trend in the mark-yen relationship? Does this shift mean that Japanese prices will rise, or that German prices will fall? Should the British company focus marketing pressure on capturing market share from the relatively weaker Japanese, or should it concentrate on countering a move by the newly advantaged Germans? What will the currency shift mean to the competitive structure of the market?

The currency exchange rate shift, taken by itself, cannot provide the answers to any of these questions. However, what has happened to exchange rates can provide a clue to what alternative opportunities are now open for the German and the Japanese competitors of this British manufacturer.

No respectable American marketing manager would make a decision on price strategy without looking at what the competition is doing. But when the competition is Japanese, that means looking at the yen. A shift in the dollar-yen relationship can torpedo any price strategy that ignores currency risk.

Here's how: If the dollar strengthens against the yen, it means that one dollar buys more yen than it bought before. It means that a Japanese competitor can charge a lower price in dollars and still have the same amount of yen to pay the factory workers in its headquarters plant near Mount Fuji. The world financial markets have effectively offered the Japanese manufacturer a chance to cut prices. And the American manufacturer has become less competitive. His costs are in dollars. Although it may not cost any more dollars to pay the factory workers in Milwaukee, it does cost more yen. That is, each dollar paid to those workers is worth more yen. Therefore, in yen terms, the American product is more expensive. The Japanese product, measured by yen, has not changed in cost, but measured by dollars, it has decreased in cost because the yen has decreased in dollar value. If the Japanese exporter keeps yen prices constant, then the dollar price of the Japanese product falls. The American manufacturer may not at first realize that he is less competitive because he may not realize that the value of the dollar is only a function of the value of the yen. He may only recognize that currency is a competitive force when he sees a Japanese competitor gobbling up market share.

During the first term of the Reagan presidency, the U.S. dollar strengthened steadily, gaining value day by day, marking new height after new height, year after year. Despite their best efforts at cost cutting, many American manufacturers could not compete with foreign producers, and they lost market share. The Rust Bowl looked rustier than ever. Serious academic treatises warned of the deindustrialization of America, and the hound of trade war nearly snapped his leash. Politicians rallied to beat back the foreign import tide with the reed of protectionist legislation. The Japanese trade surplus surged. In Europe, where companies selling to the United States saw their dollar receivables gain value day by day, a banker told *The Wall Street Journal* that "everyone is laughing all the way to the bank."

Then, as abruptly as it had risen, the dollar turned down. From April 1985 until the autumn of 1986, it fell steadily, then slowed, then fell again in 1987. By April 1988, the dollar had slid 35 percent in real terms against other major currencies. In Japan, the currency shift caused a number of so-called high-yen bankruptcies. Small- and medium-size Japanese companies who supplied the big Japanese exporters found their customers buying less, in part because the exporters were exporting less, in part because the exporters were looking for cheaper suppliers in countries whose currencies were linked to the weak dollar. Korean imports to Japan boomed, putting pressure on small, domestic Japanese suppliers. Japanese manufacturers of lower-technology, labor-intensive items could no longer compete in export markets with manufacturers in developing or newly developed countries.

On the other side of the world, the German airline Lufthansa lost well over $100 million trying to hedge the dollar cost of airplanes it had purchased from Boeing. Thousands of steelworkers were thrown out of their jobs in the Ruhr valley, in part because the strong mark made German steel uncompetitive internationally. The chairman of Porsche resigned abruptly, under pressure, because he had focused his strategy on the American market when the dollar was high; but now that the dollar was low, Porsche could only maintain unit sales levels by sacrificing margin and slashing profitability. In the United Kingdom, Jaguar had the same problem. Jaguar's difficulties eventually led to a takeover bid by Ford in 1989.

Currency Risk and the Bottom Line

Meanwhile, U.S. exports boomed. By 1988, *The Wall Street Journal* wrote that Cummins Engine Company was running plants on three shifts. Other observers warned that American manufacturers were approaching the limits of capacity. But the Americans were not laughing all the way to the bank—not all of them, anyway. Some American companies had learned their lesson well during the difficult years of dollar strength and were paying close attention to currency risk. When the dollar fell, they asked themselves how much of their new success was simply a transient effect of the currency markets.

In fact, currency risk was one of a number of factors that had caused problems for U.S. companies. In the case of Caterpillar, for example, Komatsu had come to market with hydraulic excavators, and this product enjoyed a very good reception. Caterpillar was not particularly strong in hydraulic excavators at the time. Komatsu also had a substantial price advantage because of the strong dollar during the early 1980s. Precise quantification of how much of Caterpillar's difficulties during the early 1980s came from failure to manage currency risk, how much from labor strife in Peoria, and how much from the wrong decisions on product mix may not be possible. Where companies have managed to quantify the impact, they are generally unwilling to release the information because they consider it to be proprietary competitive data. Caterpillar is especially tight-lipped in this respect. But a careful investigator can learn that foreign exchange gains accounted for $100 million of Caterpillar's revenues in 1986. In fact, without these gains, Caterpillar would have suffered a $24 million loss that year instead of a reported $76 million profit. So, although Caterpillar's top management no longer blames currency moves as the bogey responsible for the effects of management errors in marketing and manufacturing, currency is still an important concern. That is why Caterpillar was one of the first American companies to establish an interdisciplinary group of operating and financial personnel to define and manage the effects of currency risk.

U.S. auto makers also used to complain vociferously about the undervalued yen. During the period of dollar strength in the early 1980s, Chrysler's competitive analysis team determined that about 60 percent of the cost of a Japanese vehicle sold in North America was yen cost so that a 30 percent change in the yen-dollar rate would change the cost (expressed in dollars) of that Japanese vehicle by 18 percent, a 40 percent change, by 24 percent, and so forth. The same Chrysler analysts pored over the annual reports of Japanese auto makers and calculated that Japanese producers enjoyed a production cost advantage of approximately $2,000 per vehicle.

This production cost advantage came partly from more efficient Japanese management and production methods, partly from currency advantages. It was not possible to quantify the precise contribution of each factor. Only if the Japanese had had exactly similar plants in the United States and in Japan, with exactly similar workers—that is, plants exactly similar in all variables except currency, so that the only uncontrolled variable was currency—only then could anyone assert with precise quantitative certainty the exact contribution of currency advantages to the cost advantage of Japanese manufacturers.

Although currency risk may elude precise quantification because of the presence of other cost and performance factors that cannot be separated with scientific certainty, it became clear to the American companies discussed in this book that currency risk was important. Therefore, they undertook to study their experiences during the lean, mean years and to implement strategies for the management of currency risk.

What This Book Is About

This book tells the story of what they learned, how they learned it, what they did, and what they are doing about management of currency risk. The companies whose stories are told here have learned that *risk* is really a compound word, a word that may also be spelled *threat-opportunity*. These companies have experimented with a variety of approaches to protect themselves against the threat contained in currency risk without sacrificing the opportunity. They recognize that currency shifts affect their marketing, purchasing, and manufacturing costs. They have analyzed the ways in which currency shifts affect them, and they have decided to address the issue of currency risk systematically. Their approaches differ one from the other: One trades currencies actively, for profit; another locks in the dollar value of every nondollar receivable with forward contracts. The approaches differ because of different levels of sophistication in management's understanding of currency risk, different competitive structures in each industry, different degrees of tolerance for uncertainty and surprises in reported earnings, and different degrees of confidence in the efficiency of markets.

Therefore, this book is not about the one best way to manage currency risk but about what the avant-garde of American companies are doing to manage currency risk. Here, the managers themselves explain in their own words why they have decided to do what they do. This is not a book about options pricing theory or about trading futures or about economic forecasting. Nonetheless, some of these companies use financial contracts, in particular currency options and currency forwards, to solve marketing or purchasing problems—operational problems not usually thought of in connection with banks and foreign exchange traders. They also use operational measures, such as purchasing or pricing decisions, to address the financial issue of currency risk. From the decisions and the learning processes of these companies, from their reasons for doing what they do, the reader can learn to ask useful questions about his or her own business. The use of financial instruments, especially, is a subject that lends itself to a variety of treatments.

In this book, I am not much concerned with the pricing or the technical characteristics of instruments. There are many books that explain in fascinating mathematical detail the curious quirks of financial tools, and those books can be as absorbing as a study of the laws of thermodynamics. This book is more like a Boy Scout Handbook that shows the reader several ways to build a campfire and stay warm without burning down the forest. The approach here is descriptive, rather than normative.

Currency Contracts as a Marketing Tool:
FMC Experiment

FMC Corporation, for example, is a multinational producer of machinery and chemicals for industrial, agricultural, and defense applications. Headquartered in Chicago, FMC in 1988 operated eighty-eight manufacturing facilities and mines in fifteen countries. Roughly one third of FMC's $3.3 billion in 1988 sales derived from international markets.

In the first half of 1988, an Irish chemical subsidiary selling microcellulose to aspirin manufacturers in the European market had been enjoying a substantial marketing advantage thanks to a weak dollar. At the time, FMC had been pricing the product in dollars. As the value of the dollar went up and down, the price to the European customers went up and down as well. European aspirin makers sold their aspirins to European headache sufferers (of whom there were more than a few at the time, especially among the managers of European companies that had to compete with the weak U.S. dollar), who paid for their aspirin in European currencies. The European aspirin makers bought microcellulose from FMC, and paid for it in local currencies. However, the amount of local currency paid changed according to currency exchange rates between the dollar and the local currency. When the dollar strengthened, the aspirin maker wrote a bigger check in marks, francs, or lira. When the dollar fell, the check was smaller. The volatility of the dollar, which rose and fell unpredictably, made planning more difficult for aspirin makers, who could not be confident of their cost projections because their costs were dependent on an unpredictable relationship between the U.S. dollar and their home currency. Furthermore, it was clear that a long period of dollar strength would favor FMC's European competitors in the microcellulose business.

FMC had prepared a forecast of estimated sales for the Irish subsidiary, and laid this forecast alongside an exchange rate forecast for the U.S. dollar. FMC's treasury staff concluded that the dollar would probably strengthen over time. And its marketing staff knew that a strong dollar would spell pricing trouble for the Irish subsidiary. Market intelligence was already reporting competitive threats. Instead of planning to meet the competitive threat by cutting prices and sacrificing margins, FMC decided to fight the battle with financial weapons. To prevent the expected strengthening of the dollar from hurting sales in Europe, FMC went to the currency markets. Because sales of microcellulose had been fairly constant over time, the company sold European currency revenues forward at an attractive dollar rate. The forward contract covered that portion of the sales forecast that seemed, in light of past sales history, certain to be realized. For the remainder of the forecast sales, FMC purchased currency options to hedge against a strengthening in the dollar. These options entitled FMC to convert European earnings to dollars at favorable rates. Through this combination of financial instruments, the company locked in the attractive exchange rate and ensured price stability for three years. It was then possible for FMC to maintain prices in local currencies while retaining the competitive advantage of a weak dollar despite the dollar's subsequent strength.

FMC is not alone among American companies in using financial risk management tools to help operating units meet their business challenges. Monsanto, the multinational chemical manufacturer headquartered in St. Louis, has used currency options to ensure that its operating units will meet or exceed budget targets despite possible currency exchange rate shifts. However, Monsanto has not hedged beyond a budget period—about one year. FMC's hedge, as outlined in the above example, went out three years, but a long-term forward hedge can be dangerous if it is not carefully monitored and managed.

Financial Hedge Instruments: Benefits and Disadvantages

Forwards

FMC's hedge had two components: a forward component and an option component. According to the terms of the forward contract, FMC was obliged to deliver a set amount of European currency in return for dollars at a future date. The rate at which the exchange would take place, *the forward rate*, was the price. Regardless of what happened to the value of the dollar, FMC would only receive the contracted dollar price for the European currencies that it was obligated to deliver. If the price at which FMC had agreed to exchange currencies continued to be favorable, FMC would profit on the currency exchange. That is, FMC's European currency revenues would be worth more dollars thanks to the forward contract than they would be worth at spot market rates. Dollars gained on the currency contract could offset disadvantages that would arise if the dollar strengthened against European currencies. FMC could set its prices in European currencies and know that when it exchanged those currencies for dollars, it would receive a dollar price that was excellent by historical standards.

A *forward agreement* is a contract to exchange currencies. Banks do not charge a premium for forward contracts; they make their money on the difference between the rate at which they will buy a currency and the rate at which they will sell. This difference is called the *bid-offer spread*. Because banks do not charge a premium for forwards, some companies consider the forward to be an inexpensive way of hedging. This is not always the case.

FMC knew with certainty the dollar price it would receive for its European currency revenues. However, knowing with certainty a future dollar price for European currencies does not remove all uncertainty of exchange rate shifts. If the FMC treasury staff had been wrong about their outlook for the dollar—if instead of strengthening, the dollar had weakened precipitously—FMC would have had to sell European currencies for fewer dollars than they were worth in order to honor the terms of the forward contract. There would have been a substantial opportunity cost.

Perhaps the most renowned example of a company that got caught in this trap is Lufthansa, whose sad story occupied many columns in the world financial press during 1986. Lufthansa had contracted for the purchase of aircraft from Boeing in the United States. The purchase was denominated in dollars. Lufthansa's revenues were mostly in nondollar currencies. The company's financial staff forecast that the dollar would become stronger. In order to ensure that Lufthansa would not have to pay more European currency for the dollars it would require to settle the bill for the aircraft, Lufthansa decided to buy dollars forward. However, instead of rising, the dollar fell—fast and far. Lufthansa lost in the neighborhood of $140 million on this hedge, and the company's chief financial officer lost his career because of this error.

Britain's *Economist* magazine had made a similar mistake in 1984, which *The Wall Street Journal* reported somewhat gleefully. *The Economist* receives a large stream of revenues in dollars from sales in the United States. Because *The Economist*'s financial staff expected the dollar to weaken, they decided to sell their dollar revenues forward for pounds. However, instead of weakening, the dollar strengthened. Instead of making a gain, *The Economist* made a loss. "The British business weekly *The Economist* often preaches to readers about how to manage their money," *The Wall Street Journal* wrote at the time, adding insult to injury. "Now comes word it doesn't always do so well with its own cash."

From these examples, it may be seen that forward contracts do not eliminate currency risk. They guarantee a price, but there is no way of being sure that the price will be a favorable one. FMC undertook its hedge on an experimental basis, however, and manages its currency exposures actively. It can be risky to hedge with a forward, especially over a long time period, if a company does not carefully monitor the position or if the company ignores clear market trends and does not "unwind" the position when it becomes dangerous. However, companies can minimize losses by prudent management strategies. In FMC's case, this hedge was part of a broad experimental program to discover how currency exposures could best be managed. Other aspects of this experiment included treating currency exposures as a portfolio in order to maximize their value, enhancing income by writing (selling) options on currencies and generally attempting to benefit from arbitrage opportunities and exchange rate moves by trading currencies as a bank trades them.

A company with this active an approach to currency management is unlikely to take on a long-term forward hedge without monitoring it closely and changing it when change is necessary. The key to success here is having the humility and honesty to accept that one may have made a wrong decision on rates and having a consequent alacrity to correct one's mistake by unwinding the forward hedge, even if it means taking a small loss. Small losses are not good, but they are preferable to large losses. This strategy will receive more detailed attention in the discussion in Chapter 6 of Union Carbide, another active currency trader that attempted to make money on its currency positions.

Options

Besides the risk that one has guessed wrong about the direction of currency moves and locked in an unfavorable price by selling or buying currencies forward, there is a second kind of risk that comes with hedging future revenues on the forward market. This is the risk that the sales will not be made and that European currency revenues will simply not be there. If for some reason the sales forecast had been wrong, then FMC would have had to purchase European currencies on the open market so that it could have delivered them to the bank in order to settle its obligation under the forward contract.

That is why FMC did not hedge its entire sales forecast using forwards: Because some portion of the forecast sales might not occur, FMC did not commit to sell those revenues forward. Instead,

FMC purchased an option. The currency option gave the company the right to exchange European currencies for dollars at a fixed price but did not put FMC under any obligation to make this exchange. If the forecast sales did not occur, or if exchange rates moved and the price was no longer attractive, FMC could walk away without any obligation.

Options, unlike forwards, cost money. The price of an option is called a *premium*, and this premium is often compared to an insurance premium. A company that purchases fire insurance on its plant pays a premium. If the plant burns to the ground, the company receives money from the insurance company. If the plant does not catch fire, the company receives no money, nor does it get the premium back. (The question of whether the company is better off with a plant that has burned to the ground or with an intact plant is beyond the scope of this book. No doubt, the answer varies according to circumstances, and it is certainly true that different companies have resolved this question in different ways.)

Similarly, a company that purchases a currency option pays a premium for protection against exchange rate events that may or may not occur. If currency exchange rates move unfavorably, the company may *exercise* the option, making the exchange to which it has purchased the right. If, on the other hand, currency exchange rates do not move unfavorably, the company has paid for an option premium that cannot be recovered.

Another point must be noted: Financial hedges are temporary things. Whether a company hedges revenues with forwards or with options, a financial hedge provides protection only over a limited period of time.

For the past several years, popular wisdom has said that America educates too many "paper shufflers" and not enough "metal benders." Newspapers, television personalities, and candidates for political office have clambered onto the bandwagon, decrying useless financial instruments. In fact, America now leads the world in the development and implementation of innovative financial instruments. Some of the brightest minds in physics have shifted their attention to economic analysis and the development of new financial weapons for the currency wars. Financial engineers speak in terms of stochastic processes and differential equation techniques. Formidable mathematicians have taken up the challenge—men such as Fischer Black of the investment bank Goldman Sachs, a former professor at MIT's Sloane School of Management, who conducted seminal work on the analysis of options pricing. Yet for all of the progress that has been made in the development of financial weapons, it remains true in practice that such devices only provide temporary cover. Temporary shelter is good to have, but eventually even well-hedged companies have to face the real economic facts of life without the shelter of a financial hedge. In subsequent chapters, we will see how some American companies have learned to walk on two legs, the leg of financial hedges and the leg of operating measures, as they address currency risk.

I have noted briefly the example of FMC, which used a financial tool to achieve a marketing objective. However, FMC did not rely entirely or exclusively on financial tools. Note that the manufacturing plant that serves the European market is in Ireland. According to FMC's treasury staff, this plant uses a combination of American and European materials. If the dollar strengthens, the cost of labor and the cost of European materials will not change in European currency terms. Only that portion of costs that derives from U.S. dollars will change in European currency terms. By manufacturing in Europe, FMC has established a partial *natural hedge*, an operating measure that matches costs and revenues. By adding the benefits of financial engineering to this natural hedge, FMC may be able to protect itself fully against temporary exchange rate moves and even profit from them.

Operating adjustments and natural hedges are not always the same thing. An adjustment to operations, typically a change in prices or a change in costs through retrenchment, may help a company to weather changes in currency exchange rates that affect the bottom line. However, it is not usually desirable to make price or cost decisions on the basis of volatile, unpredictable exchange rates. Hedging exists in order to give stability to earnings and to make these operating adjustments less imperative.

Let's take a brief look at how Japanese companies use operating measures to protect themselves against adverse currency moves.

Operating Measures to Address Currency Risk

Richard C. Marston of the University of Pennsylvania Wharton School investigated pricing patterns of Japanese manufacturing companies both in the export and in the domestic Japanese markets. He published his findings in a working paper of the National Bureau of Economic Research in March 1989. Based on analysis of price data from 1980 through 1987, Marston concluded that "the evidence strongly suggests that Japanese firms vary their export prices relative to their domestic prices in response to changes in real exchange rates." That is, when the yen becomes strong (expensive), Japanese manufacturers raise their domestic prices while keeping their export prices constant. When the yen becomes weak, they raise their export prices while keeping the domestic prices constant. Because the Japanese market is virtually off-limits to foreign exporters, Japanese manufacturers can use domestic sales to subsidize export pricing strategies, Marston says.

Japanese pricing behavior in the home market is an operating adjustment that helps mitigate the effect of currency rate shifts on foreign currency prices of Japanese exports. All other things being equal, particularly market access, Japanese exporters would have to raise prices on exported goods in order to maintain margins when the yen strengthened. However, if prices in the domestic market can go up without fear of foreign competition, price adjustments in the export markets can enjoy at least a partial subsidy. Of course, the Japanese home market cannot subsidize export prices forever. The export market is a much bigger market for most Japanese exporters. The home market cannot absorb all of the effects of a pronounced, prolonged strengthening of the yen. Eventually, export prices have to rise. Otherwise, costs would have to be reduced or margins sacrificed. Japanese manufacturers therefore do more than rely on the captive home market to subsidize export prices when the yen strengthens.

One common operating hedge is to match the currency of costs with the currency of revenues. If the costs and revenues are both in dollars, then there is no mismatch between the two. A strong yen presents no problem to a Japanese manufacturer who pays for materials, labor, and other costs in dollars. On the contrary: When the yen strengthens, the Japanese manufacturer who pays in dollars benefits from the weakness of the dollar and remains on an equal footing with American manufacturers as far as currency advantage is concerned.

There are two ways that Japanese companies have achieved or approached this match. One is to purchase more components and materials from countries whose currencies rise and fall together with the dollar. Korea and Taiwan, for example, have long pegged their currencies to the dollar. Japanese companies purchasing from Korean and Taiwanese manufacturers, among others, reap the benefits of matching by proxy the currency of costs and the currency of revenues. The Korean won and the Taiwanese NT dollar, pegged to the U.S. dollar, rise and fall in value as the dollar rises and falls. As long as the won and the NT dollar are pegged to the U.S. dollar, the manufacturer in Korea or Taiwan benefits from a weakening of the U.S. dollar with respect to the Japanese yen because his own currency also weakens in relationship to the yen. What's more, if other costs in Korea and Taiwan are lower than costs in the United States, a weakening of the U.S. dollar makes suppliers in Korea and Taiwan even stronger competitors for Japanese purchase orders. As we will see in Chapter 3, this phenomenon was at the heart of a surprising failure by American exporters to capture Japanese market share when the dollar tumbled after 1984.

But the most visible and effective means to neutralize currency risk has been for Japanese companies to establish manufacturing facilities in the United States. When the yen is relatively weak, Japanese automobile manufacturers can manufacture cars in their domestic plants, servicing their domestic market and exporting to the United States. When the yen is relatively strong (and the dollar relatively weak), it becomes more economical to manufacture cars in the United States. Japanese manufacturers with plants in both Japan and the United States can be winners whichever way currencies move. A Japanese auto maker with plants in the United States can enjoy more attractive margins on its domestic Japanese sales by exporting cars from North America to Japan when the yen is strong, thereby enhancing its competitive position with respect to other Japanese car companies that manufacture in Japan for the Japanese market. At the same time, a Japanese auto maker who manufactures in the United States incurs dollar costs that neatly hedge its dollar sales.

An operating measure that matches costs and revenues is called a *natural hedge*. Japanese auto makers are not the only Japanese companies to have used natural hedges in the U.S. market. During the first half of 1986, a number of Japanese electronics companies announced acquisitions, new plant construction, or expansion of their manufacturing facilities in the United States. The list included Sony, Kyocera, Mitsubishi Metal Corp., NEC, and Matsushita Electric Industrial Company.

*   *   *   *   *

Currency risk is part of every business. More than just a financial concern, currency risk can determine the success of pricing, purchasing, and plant siting strategies. There are many ways to address currency risk. They may be divided roughly into three categories: financial hedges, operating (natural) hedges, and operating adjustments. *Financial hedges* include currency forwards and currency options, among others. They provide useful, temporary protection against adverse exchange rate moves. *Natural hedges* and *operating adjustments* may be more long-term in nature. Japanese companies have made extensive use of both operating adjustments and natural hedges in their approach to the U.S. market. To some extent, Japanese companies have subsidized their export price strategies using the domestic market (an operating adjustment), but they have also increased their sourcing from countries whose currencies are pegged to the U.S. dollar, and they have invested in the United

States (both are natural hedges). To the extent that they match dollar costs with dollar revenues, Japanese companies hedge the risk of an adverse movement in the yen-dollar rate.

Not all of the operating measures used by Japanese companies would work for non-Japanese companies. Differential pricing—that is, maintaining a higher price in the home market than in foreign markets—did not work for American managers during the period of dollar strength in the first Reagan administration. It did not work, in part because imports into the United States are easy. Companies that attempted to maintain differential prices found themselves competing with entrepreneurs who bought a product overseas where it was cheap, brought it back to the United States, and sold it at a profit while still managing to undercut the original manufacturer who was attempting to maintain differential prices. This *grey market* made differential pricing difficult. Furthermore, it is much easier for foreign manufacturers to sell in the United States than for foreign manufacturers to sell in Japan. When the dollar strengthened, therefore, a rush of cheap imports captured U.S. market share. U.S. manufacturers were under pressure, and could not easily maintain high domestic prices in their home market. Despite the strength of the yen, large Japanese manufacturers have not suffered as greatly from the pressure of imports—a fact attested to by the Japanese balance of trade.

Although differential pricing on the Japanese model may not be practical for American or European businesses, nonetheless, the natural hedges that come from a matching of currency costs with currency revenues can be used by non-Japanese as well. In Chapter 8, we will see how Digital Equipment Corporation and IBM have both attempted to achieve this type of natural hedge position. We will also examine how some companies have integrated natural hedges with financial instruments to protect their businesses or to generate extraordinary gains.

CHAPTER 2

A Guide for the Perplexed

Union Special: The Gambler

Union Special, a small sewing machine manufacturer based in Chicago, had been in business nearly one hundred years before it was acquired by a Japanese competitor in 1988. Controlled by the heirs of the founder, Union Special had averaged around $100 million in sales per year. A conservative company, Union Special did not trade actively in the currency markets. However, management effectively bet the entire company on one possible outcome of floating exchange rates. At the time, management did not know that it was betting the company's independent existence on the level at which the dollar had traded for a short while in the mid 1970s. Even today, those managers who still remain with the company say that the decisions on manufacturing and pricing were good ones—

21

good decisions undone by a powerful external force that hit many similar companies at the same time. Edward O'Connell, Union Special's CFO, says:

> We had some difficulties back in the early 1980s, like most American manufacturers who primarily made product here but sold it worldwide. We do 50 percent of our sales overseas, yet we manufacture maybe 80 percent of our product here. So when the dollar started to get strong, we had a tough time.

Union Special manufactured in Germany and the United States. However, German facilities were small. They never accounted for more than a quarter of capacity. In the 1970s, the company decided against a dual source production system, although that would have given it a partial natural hedge by establishing more extensive manufacturing facilities in Europe in order to serve the European market. So when the dollar strengthened in the early 1980s, Union Special had to tighten its belt. The company decided that it was more important to remain in the market than to retain margins and developed a schedule of discounts for foreign customers. "Obviously," says O'Connell, "it had a very negative effect on profits."

Instead of manufacturing in Europe for the European currency market and in the United States for the dollar market, Union Special decided to concentrate almost all of its manufacturing in the United States. This meant that Union Special had decided to incur almost all of its costs in dollars. Yet half of the company's sales went to customers who conducted their own businesses in currencies other than the dollar. Union Special's manufacturing decision was a decision to mismatch currency costs and currency revenues. By deciding to concentrate manufacturing in the United States, its management made an implicit assumption that the dollar would remain pretty stable against other currencies.

During the mid 1970s, the dollar was quite weak. However,

Union Special decided to run its business as if then-current exchange rates were fixed.

They weren't. During the early 1980s, the dollar strengthened massively. Union Special had a choice: It could maintain dollar prices to cover dollar costs, which decision would have priced its product out of the market, or it could sacrifice margins by cutting prices in dollar terms. Union Special took the latter path.

The company's stock had always traded at a discount-to-book value, and earnings erosion during the strong dollar years did not help. The sharks began to circle in 1986. In 1987, the death of Union Special's chairman put the controlling block of shares on the market, and an Australian takeover entrepreneur snapped up 30 percent of the company. It was a bargain. There were eager buyers in Japan. In 1988, Union Special ceased to exist as an independent company.

Like many companies, Union Special was unprepared for the competitive challenge it had to face when the dollar soared, and the company's difficulties were reflected in the stock price. Union Special's management should have established dual sourcing instead of concentrating its costs in the United States. A plant in Europe would mean costs in European currencies; the dollar's strength would not have hurt European sales or margins if Union Special had taken this course.

Union Special should have been prepared to switch sourcing when the dollar moved up. Many of its customers were apparel makers in Asia. When the dollar moved up against the yen, the Japanese competitive advantage in the Asian markets, formidable even in the best of times, became insuperable. Yet if Union Special had taken action early to diversify its currency cost base, the company could have managed the dollar's run-up by natural hedges. Instead, management chose to deny itself these alternatives. By concentrating virtually all manufacturing in the United States, management bet the company on a short-term trading level of the U.S. dollar.

Management made the wrong bet.

Know Thyself

Currency risk is a curious kind of risk. In some companies, it is critically important. In others, it may safely be ignored. However, the choice of whether to pay close attention to this risk or to ignore it ought to be based on a thorough understanding of how currencies affect the business. A number of consulting firms, banks, and other service companies now offer help to companies interested in getting a better handle on their currency risk.

Abe George, for example, is president of Multinational Computer Models Inc. (MCM), a management information systems company providing software for foreign exchange exposure analysis and risk management. His approach emphasizes the competitive and operational effects of currency risk: "The real issue is that you want to sell your products globally, you want to sell at a profit. How is foreign exchange risk going to hinder you or help you?"

MCM offers off-the-shelf computer programs that keep track of currency exposures and hedge portfolios. It also claims to be the world's largest commercial carrier of historical foreign exchange rates. Using MCM's data base of historical exchange rates, customers can check present exchange rate moves against similar moves in the past in order to forecast and manage currency effects on their businesses. George believes that such information is necessary in order to manage currency risk effectively.

At EMCOR, another risk management consulting firm, the trading of currencies receives far less emphasis than operating measures. EMCOR examines the overall risk profile of a client, not only volatile currency but also interest-rate, or energy price, effects on the business.

Still another perspective comes from banks and brokerage houses, many of whom offer pricey "black boxes" to solve putative problems.

As companies have become more aware of currency risk and its possible effects on business, the market for products and services is swelling. Now, an army of salesmen and savants is pounding its way through the carpeted corridors of corporate America. Some sell

colorful software programs; others hawk innovative financial transactions that, when graphed, resemble aerial photographs of lost
cities. But the best advice for managers beginning to look at their
currency risk is that given in ancient Greece to the disciples of the
peripatetic philosophers: "Know thyself."

Managers ought first to collect basic information about the
nature of their exposures and the general effects of currency moves
on business. This information can be obtained easily and inexpensively through informal, low-tech asking around. The product or
area manager knows who the most dangerous competitors are, what
happens to pricing and market share when currencies move, and
whether costs in general and currency costs in particular can or
cannot be passed on easily. Purchasing managers know from whom
they are buying, and should know how currency values are treated
in purchase contracts—if they are treated at all. The purpose of the
initial exercise is simply to gather gross, broad-brush indications of
whether a company has a currency risk and, if so, what kind of risk
it is.

Once this information is at hand, managers should decide
whether, in general, the risk can be managed through operating
responses. Can sources of supply be shifted or diversified to reduce
the threat of price increases due to appreciation of any single
currency? If the vendor is an importer, can the purchasing manager
negotiate an arrangement to share cost reductions that come about
because of currency depreciation in the country where the importer
is sourcing the product? After all, financial hedges only provide
temporary protection to facilitate operating adjustments. Sooner or
later, currency risks must be addressed on an operating level.
Therefore, it is best to consider first what operating responses the
company may be in a position to take and to consider financial
hedges as a last resort, something that hedges the superfluous risk
that cannot be eliminated through other means.

Information about financial instruments and their application
is generally available either from banks or through moderately
priced seminars. The Philadelphia and Chicago options exchanges
both conduct classes on how to use currency options. Commercial

and investment banks active in foreign exchange markets also offer classes, conferences, and other occasions for gathering information on the subject. However, most banks are in the business of foreign exchange to make money and, as a rule, only make money if and when they sell transactions. This natural bias may from time to time color their presentations. And, while transactions are not necessarily undesirable (and may indeed be quite desirable), nonetheless, the decision of whether or when to use financial hedges is one of the final decisions to be made in a currency risk management program.

Deciding How to Manage the Risk

The approach to currency risk should be driven by and compatible with the company's approach to managing the overall business. This approach may be determined largely by the nature of the industry and economic environment in which the company operates.

For example, pharmaceutical companies do not generally suffer from competitive currency risk. Production cost is a minor component of the price of a drug, and price is usually not the determining factor in a customer's decision to buy a particular medication. Nor is price competition very important. In most markets, pharmaceutical prices are controlled. Therefore, the currency risk profile of a pharmaceutical company looks very different from that of an automobile manufacturer. The primary impact of currency shifts on a pharmaceutical company is on the U.S. dollar value of foreign currency sales.

But for the automobile manufacturer, cost is an important part of the pricing decision. Automobiles tend to be positioned against each other by competing manufacturers, and price is part of the positioning. Prices of automobiles are not controlled in most markets, and consumers take price very much under consideration when they make their purchase decision. Automobile manufacturers consider currency values when they make decisions on where to source components and how to draft purchasing contracts. The cost effect of currency values may far outweigh any other currency risk for an auto maker.

In the case of a large U.S. consumer goods manufacturer that sells a popular, name brand comestible in many countries, local advertising, distribution, and other local costs may account for nearly 80 percent of the price to the consumer. Only one component of the product may be imported from the United States, and this component accounts for only 20 percent or less of the price to the consumer. Even if the U.S. dollar strengthens by 25 percent, the consumer price needs to increase only by 5 percent to keep margins inviolate. Furthermore, because the product relies heavily on trademark acceptance, barriers to entry by new competitors are high. Even if a local competitor enjoys a substantial production cost advantage, it is difficult to win market share because advertising and brand awareness far outweigh price in the consumer's purchase decision. Although this consumer goods manufacturer has no competitive currency risk and can pass through dollar cost increases in its pricing, the treasurer nonetheless takes a very active approach to managing a portfolio of foreign currency revenue flows in order to maximize the value of the corporation.

Each of these companies has currency risk. No two risks are identical, and therefore, no one risk management approach or philosophy will answer the needs of all companies.

Companies that are just beginning an international marketing push may also have to take into consideration the fact that a serious foreign exchange loss may reverberate internally with such force as to discourage the company from pursuing opportunities in new and potentially profitable markets. Their approach to currency risk management will necessarily differ from that of a company with established operations in difficult markets, markets that will remain important regardless of hyperinflation, restrictions on profit repatriation, and economic woes. In the latter case, a long-term view may be easier to justify when funds are blocked for a five-year period, taxes cannot be paid, dividends do not come out, and, what's more, the currency depreciates massively day by day.

Operating Exposure

Revenue

If pricing is an important tool in market development, foreign exchange risk management approaches can help to shore up pricing strategy. A consumer goods company may approach a new market by establishing a low price position for the product in order to encourage widespread use. In this case, financial instruments may be helpful in ensuring that changes in currency values do not impair the profit margin.

Even so, one of the first requirements will be to understand the *exposures*. If the market is Germany, for example, will all of the revenue derive from sales in German marks, or will 20 percent of the business be coming from PXs and paid for in dollars? Or perhaps marketing has negotiated an agreement with a large drug-store chain present in Germany, Switzerland, and France so that the chain will pay for part of the shipments in French francs, part in Swiss francs, and part in German marks. In that case, the currency exposure of revenue is not strictly a German mark exposure, although shipments may be made to Germany.

Cost

A similar analysis should be conducted to identify a company's currency cost structure. There may be a one-time cost each year in a particular currency, or there may be smaller, less obvious exposures that must be ferreted out. There could be a licensing fee, a royalty, a distribution cost, or perhaps an ingredient paid for in a currency different from the ordinary currency in operations—a company manufacturing and selling toothpaste in Europe might import one of the key ingredients, paying for it in dollars. There might be packaging costs.

Or components. Take, for example, the case of a camera company that makes the lens in one country, the housing for the camera in another, and the mechanism for winding the film in a third. The camera is assembled in a fourth country. Such a situation can add up to exposures in four different currencies, or it may be simplified to one exposure, or none at all, depending on the currencies involved and the company's use of natural and financial hedges.

This process of analysis will yield a picture of the company's operating exposures. If all revenues are denominated in German marks, but all containers are coming from a supplier in Britain and paid for in pound sterling, there is a mismatch. If the British pound sterling and the German mark move out of line, the operating margin will increase or decrease. This is an operational exposure.

Budget

Budget exposures may also be subjected to analysis. If a U.S. company has a German subsidiary that accounts for half of its sales, the German mark revenues will often be translated into U.S. dollars for reporting purposes. The budget process must take exchange rates into account, and managers who are measured against a budget exchange rate may wish to remove exchange rate uncertainty from the environment. If the business is seasonal—with all sales in December and January, for example—the budget process for the coming year will be skewed if the budget exchange rate is set on the basis of the prior year's annual average rather than the exchange rate prevailing when most sales were made.

Natural Hedge

When exposures have been evaluated with some degree of certainty, operating measures should be evaluated as a means of coping with a mismatch. For a company assembling cameras for sale in Germany using shutters imported from France, the French franc exposure on the shutters may be eliminated if an agreement can be struck to pay for the shutters in German marks. Or, if a source for the shutters can be found in the Netherlands, the Dutch guilder generally moves in a closer relationship to the German mark than the French franc. If currencies cannot be precisely matched, they may be approximated, and the risk reduction is proportional to the closeness of the approximation.

Financial Instruments

Forwards

After operating responses have been addressed, it is appropriate to look at financial techniques for managing the risk. One alternative is forwards. Forwards lock in a rate of exchange, eliminating the uncertainty about the rate of exchange at which transactions will occur. However, forwards also eliminate the possibility of benefiting from favorable moves in currency relationships. The more uncertainty there is about the business or about the direction of rates, the less appropriate it is to use forwards.

Debt

However, where certainty of long-term flows is high, not only forwards but long-term debt may be used to hedge exposure. Multinationals with a steady stream of foreign earnings typically have some of their indebtedness in those currencies. The revenue stream is like an asset. Balancing that foreign currency asset with a currency-matched liability mitigates the foreign exchange risk. The foreign currency debt may be used to fund the overseas business, or the borrowings may be converted to dollars and used to fund the overall business. This strategy eliminates some of the risk of exchange rate moves. However, it may or may not be optimal to eliminate the risk.

For example, having a revenue stream in German marks during a period of sustained dollar weakness is good. German marks are getting more valuble. In such circumstances, it is better to have a dollar liability than a mark liability. However, if the mark suddenly weakens relative to the dollar, then the situation reverses itself. A company that seeks not to eliminate all risk but rather to retain the opportunity of favorable rate moves while eliminating the threat of unfavorable rate moves must pay close attention to timing. During a period of dollar weakness, it is more profitable to source in dollars and to have liabilities in dollars but assets in other currencies. During a period of sustained dollar strength, it is more profitable to source in currencies other than the dollar—to have assets in dollars but liabilities in other currencies.

Swaps

Financing costs have led some companies to consider the use of currency transactions as a competitive tool. A company that has no business in Japan but competes head-to-head with Japanese competitors may decide that the dollar is so weak relative to the yen that it can only get stronger. Such a company may choose to borrow yen when the yen is at its peak of strength and convert the yen to dollars. If the timing is right and the yen weakens, the company will have locked in an attractive funding cost advantage. This need not be accomplished by borrowing, of course. The same effect can be obtained from currency swaps.

A *currency swap* is an agreement to exchange a stream of payments in one currency for a stream of payments in another currency. The swap packages the series of payments into a single transaction. There are numerous variations on this basic theme. A *fixed-fixed swap* exchanges, for example, sterling and dollars at fixed interest rates. A *fixed-floating swap* in the same currencies might have one party making fixed payments in sterling over a five-year

period but receiving a floating payment of dollars, perhaps based on
the London Interbank Offer Rate (LIBOR), which is set every six
months. As the LIBOR interest rate rises and falls, the dollar
payments also rise or fall.

Options

Where the future course of business—or of exchange rates—is
uncertain and a binding contract is not desirable, options may be
the preferred hedging tool. An *option* is a contract wherein one
party has the obligation to act if a second party chooses to command. For example, a company may purchase from its bank an
option to buy British pound sterling. Perhaps the company is
bidding on a contract in Great Britain and has worked out its pricing
based on a certain exchange rate. The company is afraid that if the
exchange rate moves, it will suffer a loss on the contract. However,
it does not want to lock itself into a firm and binding agreement to
buy sterling from the bank because the contract may not be
awarded, and if the contract is not awarded, the company has no
need for sterling. Under these circumstances, the company decides
to pay its bank a sum of money, a premium, and the bank in return
agrees that it will sell the sterling to the company at a certain rate,
but only if the company chooses to buy them. If the contract is not
awarded, the company does not buy sterling. If it is, the company
does buy sterling. The company has paid for the right to choose.

Of course, options are used in many more circumstances than
this simple example suggests. Companies that manage their currency exposures in order to profit from them often both buy and
sell options. The premium that the company receives from selling
options is income. That income reduces the net cost of options that
the manager buys, or may simply be a way of maximizing returns
on the currency portfolio. As long as the option is not naked, the
company's only risk is that the option will be exercised. If the
option is exercised, the holder of the option will buy (or sell) the

currency from (to) the company at a rate more favorable to the holder of the option than to the company.

In some circumstances, writing (selling) options may be the preferred, most efficient means of managing an exposure. For example, a manager in the United States may have a receivable due to be collected in six months from a Canadian customer. The receivable is denominated in Canadian dollars. The U.S. manager wants to maximize the value of the Canadian dollars in US terms.

Suppose that today a Canadian dollar is worth US$.84. Suppose further that the net present value of a Canadian dollar that will be received in six months is US$.835 today. So the forward rate on Canadian dollars six months out is $.835.

The manager has three choices. The first is to do nothing: In six months, when the receivable is collected, the exchange rates of U.S. to Canadian dollars may be the same; or a Canadian dollar may be worth $US.85 at that time. On the other hand, a Canadian dollar may only be worth $US.82 in six months. Doing nothing allows the receivable to be worth the same, more, or less in U.S. dollar terms.

The second alternative is to go to the bank and sell the Canadian dollars to be received in six months. The bank pays $US.835 for each Canadian dollar. If the exchange rate in six months is better than today's rate, the company has suffered an opportunity loss. If it is worse, the manager has done well.

The third alternative is for the manager to write (sell) an option. The option may give another party the right to buy the Canadian dollars at a rate of $US.835. The manager receives a US $.5 premium. Suppose that the Canadian dollar appreciates to US$.8375 in six months. Then the party who bought the option will exercise it and pay US$.835 for Canadian dollars that are worth more on the market. From the manager's perspective, he has received US$.84 for each Canadian dollar. This is the premium plus the price for the Canadian dollars. This is more than the manager could have received from the bank in a forward contract; yet using this alternative has eliminated the complete uncertainty of doing nothing.

What happens if the option is not exercised? Suppose that the exchange rate moves so that instead of being worth US$.8375, the Canadian dollar is worth only $US.82. In this case, the party that holds the option will not exercise it. The manager then has to sell the receivable at US$.82 per Canadian dollar. However, the manager receives a total of US$.825 because he has already received US$.5 in option premium. The manager would have been better off to enter a forward contract, in hindsight. But the result is still better than if the manager had neither written the option nor entered a forward contract—that is, if the position had been left naked.

Writing options is a technique that can increase income or reduce hedging costs. Writing options can be combined with purchasing options in a hedge program. The premium income received from writing the option then offsets the premium cost of purchasing an option. The result is a hedge that protects the value of a position from deterioration, while allowing the hedger to retain some of the upside appreciation potential, at a lower cost than simply purchasing an option. This is called a *covered call strategy*, the safest of option writing strategies. Writing options on things that one does not own and has no certainty of receiving at a known cost (called *writing naked options*) is extremely speculative: The writer of the option promises to buy or to sell a currency at a fixed cost if the transaction is to another party's economic advantage. The more the transaction is to the other party's economic advantage, the likelier it is that the writer of the option will have to fulfill the obligation. On the other hand, writing options can be combined with an underlying position in the currency or an underlying option position that establishes a known maximum possible cost for the transaction and, in that case, may be both safe and profitable. Union Carbide, for example, is an active writer of options, and claims to be making money at the game. FMC also writes options as part of its currency risk management program, as does British Petroleum.

The Importance of Judgment

Currency risk management is much more than the management of financial instruments, but the financial instruments developed for the most part over the past five years have given companies more risk management alternatives. Yet financial managers not infrequently find it difficult to convince nonfinancial managers that financial instruments, especially options and option derivatives, can be used prudently. The use of these instruments does not imply speculation. In fact, few companies actively and aggressively manage their currency exposures for profit. Companies that do manage for profit often succeed in making money at currency trading, mostly because they are extremely cautious. It is possible to speculate wildly with options by writing naked calls or puts.

However, options can be much less speculative than old-fashioned instruments. Option strategies are cautious strategies, because they allow the manager to determine in advance the cost of his position. Where big losses have occurred, it is usually because management was unable to determine the cost of its strategy in advance—witness the Lufthansa example related in Chapter 1. Had Lufthansa hedged its purchase of the Boeing aircraft with options instead of with forwards, management would have known with certainty the cost of its hedge. Forwards, however, locked the company into a position whose cost was indeterminable. The more the position lost, the less willing Lufthansa management was to cut the losses and bail out of the position. Lufthansa's CFO rode his losing position to oblivion.

Many companies may safely utilize financial instruments to address a particularly troubling risk. For example, a chemical company selling into Japan expects to receive a stream of yen payment over a twelve-month period. Suppose that the yen is presently quite weak against the dollar but that the currency has been volatile and, over the course of the next twelve months, there is a strong possibility that the dollar will depreciate severely. On the other hand, there are interesting indications that the dollar could rally even further and climb far beyond its present level of strength.

What does the treasurer do? In a situation of such uncertainty, will he have access to a full range of financial tools to manage the exposure? In this case, selling all of the yen forward could eliminate uncertainty, but doing so may not be the optimum risk management tool because there is a strong possibility that the yen will appreciate. If that happens, the yen may be sold for more dollars and the company will be better off. An option may allow the treasurer to determine the worst acceptable case, and ensure that the downside is no worse than that, while retaining the ability to profit from favorable moves. The option may be costly; if the treasurer sells an option and buys another option, the cost is reduced. An alternative might be to sell forward a portion of the yen, leaving the rest unhedged, and to vary the proportion of hedged and unhedged exposures depending on the direction of rates.

The key to successful currency risk management is to understand the environment in which the company operates, understand the company's objectives with respect to foreign currency flows, and determine the mix of operating and financial measures that best enables the company to achieve that goal.

CHAPTER 3

"What Is My Risk?"

Before a company can understand how to manage risk, what instruments to use, and when, it must clearly identify and define the risks to be managed. There are basically two kinds of currency risk. One kind is easy to see. The other kind is almost invisible. Identifying a *transaction risk* is easy. The term refers to the risk that monies to be received in connection with a definite, firm, indisputable sale or financing transaction may gain or lose value. Transaction risk shows up on the balance sheet as a receivable or a payable.

Hidden Risk

Another kind of risk, called *hidden risk* because it is not easy to see, does not show up on financial statements. To identify and measure hidden risk, a company must define precisely what business it is in, understand where it sources, where it sells, how currency rates affect costs and prices, and how costs and prices affect market share.

A company that understands itself and its market must also identify the currency risk of its competitors. Where does the competition source and sell? What might happen to competitors if exchange rates were to go much higher or much lower? Would the competition reap cost advantages or disadvantages?

The importance of understanding the relative strength and weakness of competitors is difficult to exaggerate. For example, in the early 1980s, when the dollar strengthened against most other currencies, U.S. exports fell. Furthermore, because the relative price of domestic U.S.-manufactured product depended on expensive dollars, domestic U.S. product was more expensive than imports. Therefore, Americans bought more foreign manufactures. A drop in exports combined with an increase in imports created a massive trade deficit.

One result of these developments was intense pressure from U.S. business groups for a weaker dollar. For a variety of reasons, the dollar did weaken steadily after 1985. However, much to their surprise, U.S. manufacturers remained unable to penetrate some of the choicest markets. Furthermore, although imports from some foreign suppliers decreased, imports from other foreign suppliers actually grew. One reason, according to the U.S. Industrial Outlook for 1988, was that:

> Between 1985 and 1987, the decline in the dollar caused the price of U.S. goods to decline 34 percent relative to domestic goods in Japan, so that in January of 1987 the index of the dollar relative to the yen had fallen to 80 percent of its 1980 level. But many of the currencies of the Pacific Rim nations are either closely tied to or are weaker than the U.S. dollar. Consequently, the competitive position of the United States in Japan against these competitors showed little improvement. From early 1985 to the first part of 1987, the price of U.S. goods fell

only 4 percent against these other competitors, and by January of 1987 the index of U.S. goods relative to these other imports into the Japanese market was still 35 percent higher than in 1980.

Clearly, this demonstrates that failure to understand the competitive structure of the global market and the true effect of currency values can lead to ineffective business plans. Analyzing hidden risk is relatively simple for companies that have a narrow product line. However, companies that have a large number of products, with flows in different directions, must make the assessment on a product-by-product basis. At heart, it's really a matter of assessing what the rates might do to the demand for each product and what that means regarding either volume or margins. As Jeffrey Barr, a Citibank vice-president specializing in currency risk management, observes:

It's a lot of discussions in the cafeteria. It's a lot of lunches, a lot of thought, it's really getting your arms around it and appreciating that there really is a relationship between core business risk like what products to produce, how to produce them, where, whom do you sell to, and financial risk.

Companies that understand currency risk frequently change the way they manage the treasury function. If currency risk is related to the operating risks of the business, then the treasury function must be considered to be an integral part of business operations. Financial strategies, financial instruments, and treasury functions must be brought into closer relationship with operating units.

The importance of integrating finance with operations may be illustrated by the following example.

Suppose a company purchases supplies from Japan under a long-term supply contract, paying in yen. Suppose the company has no yen income but brings the supplies to a factory in Birmingham, Alabama, where the supplies account for 20 percent of the manufacturing cost of a product sold exclusively in the United States. This company's largest competitor is Japanese. The Japanese competitor manufactures in Japan but sells mostly in the United States. There are no other companies active in the market—a *duopoly*.

The company's revenue is in dollars, but this substantial supply contract is denominated in yen. Is this a currency risk, and should it be hedged?

There is certainly a risk that if the yen strengthens, the cost of the Japanese supplies will go up. But should the risk be hedged? A treasurer who makes hedging decisions on the basis of accounting statement information says yes. The company has a transactional exposure to a strong yen because, if the yen strengthens, the cost of the supplies will increase.

However, an examination of this company's competitive position reveals a much more threatening hidden currency risk. The American company has a competitive advantage when the dollar is weak against the yen because when the dollar weakens against the yen, the costs of the Japanese competitor go up in dollar terms. By the same token, the American company has a serious competitive disadvantage when the yen is weak.

Looked at from this perspective, the 20 percent of manufacturing costs that are yen costs ought not to be hedged. In fact, these yen costs constitute a partial natural hedge. If the yen weakens, these costs will fall in dollar terms, helping the American company to be more competitive. Buying yen forward to hedge these costs would eliminate this natural hedge and leave the company utterly exposed to the competitive risk of a weak yen.

Accounting Risk

Among the first steps in developing a program to identify and manage currency risk is defining the kind of risk that is most serious for the organization. This will vary from company to company. In fact, even within a company, different threats and different opportunities will be apparent to different groups. Therefore, the risk that is identified and managed may not be the risk that is of greatest economic consequence.

For example, some managers believe that accounting results are paramount. Accounting statements are seen by shareholders and creditors, and it is on accounting statements that the proverbial bottom line resides.

Accounting standards may allow for certain expenses, such as depreciation, that are not cash expenses. Assets may be reflected at historical costs rather than at market values. For various reasons, then, a company that attempts to manage threats to and opportunities for cash flow may have to take actions that do not make sense as evaluated in an accounting framework.

Sometimes, for example, companies may undertake to protect themselves against a hidden, nontransactional foreign exchange risk by using a financial hedge. Caterpillar has used forward foreign exchange contracts to lock in favorable currency rates, and FMC has done the same thing. However, present accounting standards can penalize companies that take such actions.

The accounting profession divides financial instruments into two groups: those that can be accounted for as hedges and those that cannot. In order to be accounted for as a hedge, a financial instrument must usually be matched to a firm transaction, a signed contract, a purchase order, or some other evidence that the hedge is matched against something real. Financial transactions that are not matched to firm transactions must usually be marked to market—that is, the position is considered to be a speculative investment, and its value changes from reporting date to reporting date. In a period of extreme currency volatility, a foreign currency hedge that is treated as a speculative investment causes financial statements to reflect drastic changes in value—a loss this period, a gain next period—which have no economic effect whatsoever on the company's health. Accounting standards may require that if a company hedges a large amount of "hidden" currency risk—for example, the risk from three years of anticipated (but not firmly committed) sales to be made in foreign currencies—the hedge will be marked to market and the company will seem to have very erratic earnings as the market value of the hedge rises and falls. However, the same foreign currency instruments, if they are accounted for as a hedge, reflect no change in value at all until the transaction they are hedging has been consummated. Because accountants differ in their understanding of hedging practices and in their interpretation of rules, two companies with the same hedge position and the same earnings streams may look different on financial statements simply because one company's auditor permitted hedge accounting for the position and the other company's auditor did not.

In the example above, where we observed that an American company had a small transactional exposure to a strong Japanese yen but an immense economic exposure to a weak Japanese yen, accounting standards would allow hedge accounting treatment for a financial position hedging the small transactional exposure but deny hedge accounting treatment for a financial position hedging the large economic exposure on grounds that the large economic exposure was not related to a firm transaction.

The proliferation of financial instruments over the past few years has led the accounting profession to grapple with these issues. In fact, the Financial Accounting Standards Board (FASB) is currently in the process of rewriting and redefining regulations governing financial instruments. However, the process is expected to take several years, and in the meantime, accountants differ among themselves with respect to interpreting the present rules.

Present accounting standards frequently deter companies from hedging economic risks. Reported earnings affect earnings per share, which can affect the bond rating, which certainly affects the cost of debt. So management of currency's impact on accounting results is, at some level, prudent.

Notwithstanding, companies that focus mainly on management of accounting risk are fond of saying, "Our business is to make widgets and sell widgets. Our business is not to get involved in currency speculation." Such companies generally only pay attention to the risks that will show up on quarterly accounting statements. They usually ignore or dismiss the effect of currency shifts on their long-term competitiveness. As long as they do not have to report foreign currency losses on their financial statements, they consider that they have done a good job managing exposures.

Companies that manage economic risk, on the other hand, usually believe that it is not enough to make a good appearance on the accounting statements. Instead, they attempt to make maximum use of every economic advantage that currency moves give them while protecting themselves as fully as possible against threats to their position. This type of management may seem to require considerable investment in computer systems and financial expertise. However, it need not.

Definition of Risk Determines Management

How a company defines its risk will determine how it manages the risk. Companies that define risk as risk to reported earnings typically hedge all sales when they are booked in order to avoid reporting a loss on transactions that have been booked. Companies that define risk as long-term competitive risk typically hedge selectively, using a wider variety of instruments and approaches.

Selective Hedging

A selective hedger with receivables denominated in a strengthening foreign currency does not typically lock in the present value of the receivables in his home currency through a forward transaction. Instead, if the currency in which the receivables are denominated is strengthening, the selective hedger may do nothing. For the selective hedger, doing nothing is the most dramatic possible demonstration of confidence that the direction of currency rates will increase the value of the receivables by the time they are translated into the hedger's home currency. Doing nothing is not only an action, it is an action that can only be taken when one is supremely confident that the unhedged position is going to become stronger and more valuable over time. Risk managers seldom choose to do nothing. They are not often that sure about the direction in which currencies are moving.

A manager who believes that the currency in which the receivables are denominated is unlikely to change in value, or that it will become less valuable in home currency terms (which is the same thing as saying that the home currency will strengthen), often chooses to sell the currency forward. A forward locks in the present value of the currency that will be received in the future. A forward is simply a commitment to exchange currencies at present forward market rates. The actual exchange will take place in the future. Therefore, there is an interest differential between the *spot rate,* which is the amount of currency received if the exchange is made at present, and the amount of currency received if the exchange is made in the future. Aside from this interest differential, however, there is, for accounting purposes, no cost in selling or buying a currency forward.

However, forwards are not flexible. They are firm agreements. If the exchange rate between dollars and yen is 200 yen to the dollar and a company sells yen forward at that rate, then, at the agreed future date, the company will exchange 200 yen for each dollar received. Suppose, in the meantime, the yen strengthens and the rate becomes 120 yen to the dollar. The company that agreed to exchange 200 yen for each dollar by selling forward cannot take advantage of the increased value of the yen. Therefore, the use of forwards demonstrates a high degree of confidence in the direction of exchange rates when they are used by risk managers who hedge selectively.

The selective hedger who buys or sells forward does not expect rates to get any better. By contrast, managers who manage chiefly with a view to accounting results may use forwards as a matter of course. They do so because, under present accounting rules, forwards used to hedge a firm underlying transaction lock in the book value of the sale. Of course, accounting rules have nothing to say about the real economic change, the opportunity cost that occurs when the yen moves from 200 to 120 per dollar.

For selective hedgers, doing nothing and using forwards both demonstrate a high degree of confidence in a point of view concerning currency rates. When they are less confident about their view of currency rates, these managers may choose to hedge with options. Currency options are relatively new instruments. They only came into general use in the mid-1980s. Purchase of a currency option gives a manager the right to buy or sell currency at a particular rate. However, it does not obligate him to do so. If rates get better, he may choose to let the option expire and buy or sell the currency on the market at the higher market rate.

Many managers who do not understand currency risk management consider options to be very speculative instruments. In fact, options are the least speculative of all financial instruments used for currency risk management because they do not obligate the manager to any particular course of action. A manager who does nothing is stuck with his position; a manager who sells forward is stuck without his position. The first manager keeps all of the threat and all of the opportunity. The second eliminates the threat of his position losing value, but he also eliminates all of the opportunity of his position becoming more valuable. But the manager who buys an option eliminates the threat of having his position lose value: If it becomes less valuable, he may choose to exercise the option and sell the position for more money than it is worth on the market. However, if the position becomes more valuable, he is free to hold onto it or to exchange it for more money on the market.

Hidden Risk and Laker Air

How a company defines and how well it identifies the risk posed by currency moves helps to determine purchasing and marketing decisions. Financial instruments and financial transactions are only one way of managing risk. Operating measures are also important.

Currency risk can be minuscule and not worth thinking about, or it can decide the fate of an entire company. Ignoring the risk can be costly, as Sir Freddy Laker learned to his chagrin.

British entrepreneur Sir Freddy Laker was in the business of transporting British vacationers to the United States. His marketing campaign in Britain emphasized the low cost of flying Laker for a pleasant, inexpensive holiday abroad. Sir Freddy had little difficulty filling his planes, especially when the British pound sterling was very strong against the U.S. dollar. The British felt very rich because their pounds went a long way. They could come to America and buy a lot of things cheaply. Laker's business soared.

In fact, things got so good for Sir Freddy Laker that he decided to expand. He contracted with a U.S. aircraft manufacturer to buy three more planes, and agreed to pay in U.S. dollars.

Sir Freddy received most of his revenues in British pounds from the British holiday travelers. But the U.S. aircraft manufacturer wanted payment in dollars. Therefore, in order to pay for the aircraft, he would have to sell his pounds in order to buy U.S. dollars.

This *transactional exposure*, the exposure related to the transaction of purchasing planes, can be described as a long-sterling–short-dollar position. Sir Freddy had pounds, but he needed dollars.

However, there is more to this picture than the transaction exposure. Look at the nature of Sir Freddy's business. When the pound was strong, his British customers could afford to vacation in the United States. Since Sir Freddy depended on the British vacationer and did not have much in the way of a U.S. marketing effort, his income was tied to pounds—*strong* pounds. That was also a long-sterling–short-dollar position.

Then, in the early 1980s, the pound weakened dramatically against the U.S. dollar, and the British traveler could no longer readily afford to vacation in the United States. Volume plunged, and Sir Freddy's revenues stopped coming in.

However, even though the income stopped, the outgo did not. Sir Freddy still had an obligation to sell his sterling to come up with U.S. dollars to pay for the airplanes he had bought. Now, those U.S. dollars cost more sterling, but Sir Freddy had fewer sterling coming in.

The result, of course, was bankruptcy.

Had Sir Freddy Laker carefully studied his risk, he might have discovered that he had a heavy operating or economic exposure to a strong dollar. He could have balanced, or hedged, his operating exposure by taking operating measures. For example, he could have established a serious marketing effort in the United States. Although U.S. travelers were not going overseas much when the dollar was weak, if Sir Freddy had had a foothold in the U.S. market, he would have been prepared when the dollar became strong again and Americans found that overseas travel was a bargain.

A thorough analysis of his currency risk (threat-opportunity) might also have led Sir Freddy to handle the purchase of airplanes differently. By contracting to buy planes in U.S. dollars when he had no U.S. dollar revenues and when his overall business was vulnerable to a strong dollar, Sir Freddy exacerbated his foreign exchange risk. He might have protected himself on the transaction risk by, at minimum, buying his dollars forward when he signed the contract. The forward position would not have protected him from operating exposure, but it would have protected him from the precipitous decline in the value of the pound sterling with respect to the dollar, and might have saved him from bankruptcy.

PART II

Profiles in Currency Risk Management

CHAPTER 4

Finning and Caterpillar: *Currency Risk Management for Corporate Survival*

This is the story of how currency risk shook two companies widely separated by geography and by type of business. The first company is a dealer in heavy equipment, a company with negligible manufacturing investment, little in the way of physical capital except for inventory—in short, a company that might seem almost immune to the effects of shifting currency values. Yet this company was almost destroyed by floating exchange rates.

The second company is perhaps the world's best-known name in the manufacture of heavy machinery. This company, nearly destroyed by shifting currency rates, called for government action to change the rates at which currencies traded, but

51

then discovered that a favorable change in currency values could not solve the problems that a sudden currency shock had laid bare.

Both companies now manage currency risk by a combination of operating and financial responses that have brought treasury and other corporate functions into intimate cooperation.

Finning: Challenge and Responses

The Challenge

Tumbler Ridge, in northern British Columbia, is cold and desolate country. Throughout the decade of the 1970s, it was CAT country. Mining, forestry, and road-building interests in British Columbia bought their Caterpillar equipment from Finning Tractor & Equipment Company, a fifty-three-year-old dealership whose chairman used to say, "You have to be an absolute genius to lose money as a Caterpillar dealer." That was especially true in the late 1970s, when the U.S. dollar tumbled down and the yen was strong. Finning boosted its hot 15 percent per year growth rate to an almost nuclear 22 percent per year from 1975 to 1980.

As Finning's sales grew, so did its network of branches and service centers. Service means a lot to a buyer of heavy equipment: When a big tractor goes down, it is very serious business. Time is money.

Miners, builders, and loggers knew that if they bought CAT equipment from Finning, there wouldn't be much downtime. Finning had parts stocks and trained technicians all over the province. Finning's service kept the customers loyal, and customer loyalty kept competitors out. Japan's Komatsu couldn't even break Finning's hold on the market. To go after Finning in a serious way, Komatsu would have had to establish a competitive service network. Yet Komatsu could not afford to set up a service network and stock it with spare parts, since it hadn't sold enough machines to require a service network—or to pay for one.

Finning sold CAT equipment for prices averaging about 15 percent higher than comparable equipment sold by Komatsu. When a big machine goes down, lost production and project delays can cost a lot more than 15 percent. Finning's customers paid the premium, and they figured that they got what they paid for.

Then in 1980, the dollar began a sustained, four-year rise. The magnitude of the dollar's strength may be judged by referring to an index of the dollar's real exchange rate performance against fifteen major industrial country currencies. This index, from Morgan Guaranty Trust, shows how the dollar fared in real terms, allowing for inflation differences among countries. It allows us to consider the trends in purchasing power of the dollar over this period. In January 1980, the dollar stood at 89.64 on the index. By January 1982, the purchasing power of the dollar had surged to 102.61, an increase of 14 percent in only two years. In January 1984, the index was 117.34, nearly 30 percent above the 1980 level. And by March 1985, the dollar reached its peak of strength: 131.59 on the index, or an increase of almost 47 percent above its level in 1980.

Finning's customers were Canadian. They paid Finning in Canadian dollars. But Finning sold Caterpillar equipment, imported from the United States. Caterpillar equipment was priced in U.S. dollars.

A strong dollar means that a dollar buys more. Another way to look at it is that it takes more to buy a dollar. Caterpillar hadn't raised its prices. It still sold tractors for the same amount of U.S. dollars as before. But because the U.S. dollar was stronger now, it took more Canadian dollars to pay the same U.S. dollar price. Even without a price hike, Caterpillar equipment got more expensive. In Canadian dollars, the price went up.

The strong dollar helped Komatsu to a price advantage of about 40 percent, as Finning's treasurer, P. G. von der Porten, recalls. Suddenly, Komatsu looked a lot more attractive. Caterpillar equipment had always sold at a slight premium over Komatsu, but 40 percent was far out of line.

Finning had a serious problem. Says von der Porten:

> We analyzed the situation in terms of our businesses, realizing that if we were to retain normal pricing, we would be killed because the Japanese would be able to bring in quite a few machines; and by being able to do that, getting their machine population up, they would have been able to establish large product support facilities here in BC, and having once made that beachhead, they would have been very much more difficult to compete with.

The Tactical Response

Finning management went into a huddle. The critical thing was to try to stop Komatsu. But how?

Von der Porten recalls:

> A lot of our competitors in other lines of business, not the Japanese but others, were shutting down branches and facilities throughout the province in order to cut their costs. As a deliberate strategy, we didn't choose to do that. Even if a small branch wasn't making money for us, we kept it open because we didn't want to be seen as deserting our customers in bad times. We told them this was our strategy, and this helped to hold the line.

Although he is Finning's treasurer, von der Porten has an untreasurerlike view of what the treasury function means.

> Finance and money transactions are just part of the tools that you use to run a business. They're not independent. Finance is there to run the machinery business, and the

machinery business is there to make the money. If you find that your prices are being affected by currency, it is just as much an effect as if your prices are being affected by inefficiencies in your operation. The effect on the market is exactly the same. So therefore, currency changes have to be seen in exactly that light. They are simply one other component of your pricing.

The exchange rate between the dollar and the yen had changed. That is a *financial event*. But the effect on Finning was at the operating level. The currency move hurt Finning on the logging roads and in the mines of British Columbia, where customers bought and used heavy machinery.

Out by desolate Tumbler Ridge, a huge new open-pit coal mine was starting up. Japanese financial interests owned 50 percent of that mine. The mine would need to buy a lot of machines. Because it knew that a mine of that scope could go far to establishing Komatsu in the province, Finning fought hard. It used every price break it could get from Caterpillar, and slashed its own margins down to nothing.

But with a 40 percent price advantage, Komatsu wasn't about to go away.

It was a pricing problem of considerable magnitude [von der Porten says], and it would appear that the Japanese had decided they were going to sell them tractors come hell or high water. And since there are no domestic producers of tractors in Canada, there are no provisions of the anti-dumping law that you could bring against the Japanese, so it's not a legal battle at all, it's a question of a gloves-off kind of battle.

Komatsu won. It got the tractor orders. Finning was able to beat it on a few items—some front-end loaders, some graders—but the dozer orders went to Komatsu while a German company got the order for big hydraulic shovels.

Tumbler Ridge is cold, wild country on the border of the Yukon near Dawson Creek. Finning was already bleeding red ink from the dollar-yen hit, and Komatsu was in its market now. A financial event in the currency markets, a change in the relationship between the dollar and the yen, provoked a crisis for Finning. Finning responded to this financial event with a marketing decision.

Soon, the new mine started running into problems with the German machines. Hoses snapped in the sub-Arctic cold. Finning sent technicians to fix them. The technicians installed a special hydraulic hose, metal-sheathed and reinforced, under the German shovel. "We actually serviced the hell out of them," recalls von der Porten. "We said yes, you bought these other people's machines, but you are our customer, and if we can help you in any way please let us know."

Then the mine made a discovery. Komatsu had led with a very low price for tractors, but the prices for replacement parts were anything but cheap. A tractor undercarriage is a wear-and-tear item whose replacement occurs quite frequently. The old rule of thumb was that a tractor would use its own original price every three years just in undercarriage replacements. "We're talking about a $30,000 overhaul cost in one of those tractors when we talk about an undercarriage job," von der Porten explains.

When the time came for the Komatsu undercarriages to be replaced, the customer called Komatsu, reeled at the price, and then called Finning.

> Lo and behold we found that the Caterpillar tracks fit them! It was pretty amazing that this should be, but there it was; the Japanese had built a machine that was so much like the American machine that the tracks fit, and all we had to do was do some modification to the rollers.

After the modification, the Caterpillar undercarriage fit the Komatsu machines like a glove—and it was cheaper.

By means of this marketing response, Finning managed to contain the threat that currency risk had raised. "And the moral of that was, the next machines they bought were Caterpillar," von der Porten says.

The Strategic Response

Currency risk does not only affect huge multinational corporations. Finning Ltd. is an independent business: It is considerably smaller than Caterpillar; it manufactures very little and is a service business. Yet when the dollar-yen relationship changed, thrusting Caterpillar and Komatsu into a new competitive position, Finning had to take a close look at its own vulnerability to exchange rates. What it discovered led management to make some sharp changes in the way the company was run.

Prior to this crisis, Finning had relied on market diversification—forestry, mining, logging—to support uninterrupted growth. But in 1982, all of those markets declined, and Finning's sales plunged to 80 percent under the previous year's level. In fact, Finning's sales of new product for all of 1982 was equal to only one month's sales in 1980. To preserve the equity of the company, Finning reduced employment by half. Obviously, market diversification was no longer enough. For diversification of currency exposures and a new view of currency risk management, economic diversification would now be necessary.

The strong dollar, which had made Caterpillar equipment so expensive in the early 1980s, had left Finning exposed to a threat from Komatsu. However, the threat was accompanied by an opportunity. In the middle of 1982, two dealerships in the United Kingdom became available. Finning pursued them and completed their acquisition in the third quarter of 1983. This move meant that Finning had diversified its currency base. That is, if the Canadian dollar sales were adversely affected by an increase in value of the U.S. dollar relative to the Canadian dollar, Finning might look to its U.K. operations for better results. The Canadian dollar and the U.K. pound sterling are not linked, and the two countries' economies do not move in tandem.

The economic diversification of Finning's business also provided a buffer against recession in Canada. Through the U.K.
subsidiary, Finning pushed into Eastern Europe and Iran, increasing the diversification of its economic base. Although Finning
could not directly control or manage the effect of yen moves on
Caterpillar's prices, it could, by diversification of currency revenues,
spread its risk. The way that the yen and dollar move against the
pound sterling differs in timing, magnitude, and character from the
way that they move against each other or against the Canadian
dollar. If a unit of currency may be compared to a share of stock in
an economy, then Finning diversified its portfolio, buying into the
British and other economies.

Finning also analyzed its exposure to currency moves and
discovered an interesting thing: The rising U.S. dollar had brought
problems, but a weakening of the U.S. dollar relative to the
Canadian dollar might also spell trouble for the company. Von der
Porten explains:

> We know that if the Canadian dollar were to go up in
> value, it would have an adverse effect on Finning in two
> ways. One would be that it would adversely affect our
> customers, who are selling their coal and lumber and so
> forth in U.S. dollars. So if the Canadian dollar goes up,
> their prices go up relative to their competitors in the
> United States. The other effect it would have is that we
> have inventory that we've already paid for, and if the
> Canadian dollar suddenly rises, then we have an unreal-
> ized inventory loss.

Finning made preparations to respond to a change in currency
exchange rates on two fronts: operating and financial. The story of
Finning's victory over Komatsu, at the cost of short-term losses and
expensive strategic defenses such as servicing Komatsu's equipment,
is one example of Finning's operating response.

Finning also put its treasurer in charge of market intelligence.
Von der Porten explains:

One of the jobs which our new CEO has given me is to look after market intelligence, which is kind of an odd thing for a treasurer to be doing, but it does help me to understand what's going on in our business. In fact it's an example of how operations and treasury really come together.

P. G. von der Porten, a treasurer, helps to set Finning's marketing policies. His understanding of currency matters allows him to better analyze the strategy behind the moves taken by Finning's competitors. His responsibility for market intelligence gives him access to information about the pricing and operational decisions of Finning's competition, and makes him a valued part of Finning's marketing process.

On the financial level, von der Porten relates his borrowing practices to market developments:

If one of our customers is being hit, well it's totally off of our balance sheet, but we're taking a look at the health of our customers and saying if the Canadian dollar goes up, the health of our customers goes down, therefore in the long run our economic well-being goes down; so again it's not a strictly "financial" thing, it's part of an economic environment that you're in. So knowing that, we will structure the balance sheet in such a way that we maximize U.S. dollar borrowings rather than Canadian dollar borrowings. In other words, our U.S. sub would borrow against all its assets with U.S. debt, rather than leveraging it two-to-one or fifty-fifty or something like that. I would go full bore on U.S. borrowings. Another example along the same vulnerability would be that if we knew that we had a large payment to make in U.S. dollars to Caterpillar—next month or something like that—for $10 million, I would never buy those U.S. dollars forward, because that would only amplify our dependency on the Canadian dollar remaining low.

*   *   *   *   *

Finning's example shows how currency risk of principals can affect the business of dealers and service businesses that cannot control such basic elements of risk as manufacturing cost. However, Finning also shows that not all of the risk is uncontrollable, even for dealers. By integrating treasury with marketing, Finning has taken a small action that is under its control in order to mitigate the effects of large events not under its control. Market intelligence gleaned by the treasurer shapes Finning's understanding of currency-related competitive positioning by Komatsu in Finning's markets. Furthermore, by diversifying the economic base of sales, Finning has done on a small scale what Caterpillar, as we shall see, has done on a large scale. Ultimately, the issue of competitiveness of Caterpillar versus Komatsu will not be determined by Finning's action, and major disruptions to the competitive relationship at the manufacturing level will certainly continue to affect Finning. Yet the effects of even major disruptions will probably be less severe than they were in the early 1980s because Finning is stronger for what it has learned. What's more, the effect of smaller disruptions in currency values and competitiveness of the major manufacturers has been to some extent diversified away by Finning.

Caterpillar

Discovering the Limits of Currency Risk

Finning was not the only Caterpillar dealer to come under pressure when the yen-dollar gap opened in the early 1980s. In fact, Caterpillar lost $953 million in the 1982–1984 period. Meanwhile, the Japanese ate market share. According to securities analyst Mitchell I. Quain, who follows the heavy equipment industry for Wertheim & Co., "During the 1977–1981 period, the Japanese manufacturers increased their share of the non-Japanese market from 9 percent to 14 percent. The weak yen caused this to jump to 21 percent in 1984."

During these years, Caterpillar came to recognize the importance of exchange rates and the immense exposure of the company to the Japanese yen. Caterpillar sold relatively little to Japan, so its yen revenues were, if not negligible, certainly not of great moment. Caterpillar's direct yen expenses were similarly inconsequential. Yet when the dollar moved up against the yen, CAT nearly fell apart. Fixing currency risk management alone could not solve CAT's problem. However, in 1986, CAT booked $100 million in net foreign exchange gains. Those gains made Caterpillar's $76 million profit for the year. Without those gains, Caterpillar would have chalked up a $24 million loss.

In 1985, net foreign exchange gains had totaled $89 million, accounting for 45 percent of Caterpillar's $198 million profit for the year. Part of these gains (about $13 million in 1985—the number is not broken out in the 1986 annual report) came from forward contracts CAT had entered into in order to keep sourcing costs low. However, these hedge instruments did not all cover firm purchase contracts. They did not hedge irrevocable actions that Caterpillar had already taken but protected against currency moves that might affect actions CAT anticipated taking in the future. In other words, these contracts did not hedge Caterpillar's transactional exposures, they hedged CAT's economic and competitive exposure and allowed CAT to turn the strong dollar into a competitive advantage. CAT took the strong dollar, which had helped to make it the world's highest-cost producer, and turned it into a tool to lower the company's cost of production.

Caterpillar's long record of sales successes during the 1960s and 1970s had depended on many things: perceived product superiority, omnipresent service and distribution, strong growth in energy, and construction and mining worldwide. The so-called oil crisis of the late 1970s had helped CAT sell machines into OPEC countries, where rulers spent their petrodollar bonanza building cities, cutting roads, erecting refineries, and laying infrastructure. The developing countries of Latin America were also strong markets for CAT equipment. Banks were tripping over each other to finance projects there. The dollar was weak, interest rates were low, and money was easy. Demand for machines exceeded supply. Caterpillar continued to expand capacity. Going from success to success, CAT management looked upon its creation and found it good.

When the bubble burst in the early 1980s, Caterpillar staggered. Some observers refer to the market for heavy earth-moving equipment as a duopoly. Caterpillar and Komatsu are by far the biggest players. Throughout the 1970s, Caterpillar manufactured its product primarily in the United States, while Komatsu manufactured primarily in Japan.

Caterpillar's fate, therefore, was closely linked to the movement of the U.S. dollar. When the dollar was weak, Caterpillar sales were strong. A weak dollar meant that Caterpillar equipment was comparatively cheap. But when the dollar strengthened, the Caterpillar product became more expensive and less affordable to buyers whose revenues were in nondollar currencies. It simply took more pesos, francs, deutschemarks, yen, or rand to buy the same amount of dollars Caterpillar was charging for its machines.

Everything had been going along well. Then the dollar got strong, the yen got weak, and suddenly the walls fell in. CAT management expressed no public doubt about what the problem was. Chairman Lee L. Morgan became a familiar face in Washington, where he went to complain loudly and frequently about the strong dollar. CAT pressed the government to bring the dollar down.

The government didn't seem to listen. For CAT, though, there was no getting away from it; its business depended to a large extent on the rate at which the dollar traded. Currency risk, for Caterpillar, was an operating risk, arguably the single most potent factor of competitive life for the company. By concentrating its costs in the United States, CAT had bet the company on the continued weakness of the dollar. Then the dollar got strong.

[Caterpillar has refused to discuss for publication the details of how it identified and learned to

manage currency risk. The information that follows
was gathered from previously published reports and
a number of sources familiar with Caterpillar who
have insisted upon remaining anonymous.]

Caterpillar assembled a task force with representatives from
treasury, manufacturing, and production to study the problem and
recommend solutions. It reported directly to the top of the company. It analyzed the effect of currency moves on CAT's costs and
revenues—but went further and tried to calculate how Komatsu
would fare under the same scenarios. CAT began to look at currency
risk as a competitive advantage or disadvantage. The company
evaluated its existing manufacturing facilities and sourcing arrangements in light of what it had learned about the effect of currency
moves on competitiveness. Currency risk became a consideration
in Caterpillar's decisions about where to move production and
where to establish new sources of supply. Recognizing that a
concentration of manufacturing in the United States exposed the
company to swings in the dollar, Caterpillar started to source more
product abroad. The strategy was to diversify away from dependence
on the dollar.

The strong dollar had a threatening downside. Caterpillar's red
bottom line clearly showed that. But it had an upside as well. The
strong dollar gave CAT a true advantage in international markets.
Caterpillar could use its strong dollars to buy assets overseas—
cheaply.

For example, when the dollar had risen almost to its peak,
Caterpillar decided to move some sourcing to Europe. At that time,
the strong dollar made European products relatively cheap. However, because Caterpillar now recognized that currency relationships were very inconstant and that a fall in the dollar could make
the European supplies much more expensive in the future, the
company entered into long-term currency hedging contracts. These
hedge contracts locked in the very favorable relationship of the
dollar to European currencies. These hedge contracts did not hedge

specific purchase orders—they were essentially economic hedges. Caterpillar made sure that it would have access to cheap European product if and when needed. In fact, Caterpillar was under no obligation to buy European product at all. CAT could have merely sold its forwards at a profit, if it so chose, and applied the gains to other purposes. (We know that CAT was not using these contracts to hedge firm transactions because of the way CAT accounted for them.)

When the dollar began to fall in 1985, CAT crawled back into the black. Profit for 1985 was $198 million, compared with losses of $428 million in 1984 and $345 million in 1983. Of course, 45 percent of that 1985 profit came from foreign exchange gains, $13 million of which was gain on foreign exchange forward contracts.

Yet the company's 1986 profits slipped to $76 million—despite the fact that the dollar had weakened steadily through the year! CAT faced a dilemma. The complexity of currency risk was becoming apparent. In the first place, dollar revenues from sales in Europe were up because the dollar had weakened. But because the nondollar currencies had strengthened, all of CAT's nondollar costs were also up. Costs of manufacturing in overseas plants, selling, general and administrative costs, and any nondollar sourcing that CAT had not hedged, all cost more in dollar terms. Had CAT still not gotten its arms around the currency problem?

Investors punished the company severely. CAT shares tumbled in feverish selling. *Fortune* reacted to Caterpillar's 1986 performance as follows: "It was curious enough that Caterpillar's savvy and respected management had been so wrong about the near-term outlook. But the real mystery was why the company was doing so badly. Why hadn't it been helped by the decline in the dollar?"

It is fair to say that the currency problem had been as much a catalyst as it was a cause of Caterpillar's woes. Beleagured by a sea of troubles when the dollar had been strong, Lee Morgan and CAT management had dramatically exaggerated the importance of having a weak dollar, blaming an external force for management's own failures. Auto companies did much the same thing in the early

1980s, blaming not only currency but a whole host of allegedly unfair practices for Japan's success in the North American market.

In fact, Caterpillar's most serious problems were of the old-fashioned kind: CAT had too many plants making the wrong product in the wrong places. During the boom years, CAT had grown bureaucratic, complacent, and lethargic. Currency risk had not created these problems. Yet by creating a new and more difficult competitive situation, the upward-floating dollar had precipitated a crisis. CAT closed plants, changed the product line to give the market what the market demanded, and started to diversify sourcing and production in order to lower costs. CAT learned to use currency hedge contracts to lock in fleeting currency advantages. Results did not come immediately. Yet management's insistence during the early 1980s that currency risk was at the very heart of Caterpillar's problems had prepared some unrealistic expectations in the stock market. Management had blamed an external force for its own failures. Then, when the dollar weakened and the external force could no longer be blamed, the real problems lay exposed, like debris left behind after a flood recedes. The market responded as if the problems were new.

This story, though, has a happy ending. CAT did get to the roots of its problems. In 1987, Caterpillar's profits were up again—to $350 million. In 1988, profits jumped again—to $616 million.

CHAPTER 5

Chrysler:
When You Can't
Just Raise Prices

Chrysler is a North American company, with negligible international manufacturing or marketing. International sourcing was also negligible until recently. Therefore, in the narrow accounting sense, Chrysler had little or no exchange rate risk. Yet the company's exposure to currency moves, and especially to the Japanese yen, was significant. Chrysler, like Caterpillar, responded initially to its competitive difficulties by exaggerating the impact of apparently uncontrollable external forces, one of which was currency. However, like Caterpillar, Chrysler carefully examined this risk in the context of competitive circumstances and found a way to manage the unmanageable. This chapter lays out in

66

detail the steps Chrysler had to take to develop a risk management program suited to the needs of a company that even today remains largely based in and dependent upon the North American market.

The series of events that led to Chrysler's bailout by the U.S. taxpayer, and the company's subsequent resurgence under Chairman Lee Iacocca, seem now no less a part of home-grown Americana than Gary Cooper in *High Noon*. From Chairman Lee's direction of the Statue of Liberty Centennial show to the sustained drumroll rumbling against unfair Japanese competition, the image of Chrysler's lonely showdown against foreign competitors has undoubtedly played well in certain important Chrysler market segments.

However, the melodramatic recital of complaints against insidious Japanese competitive practices dished out for public consumption by auto industry publicists, especially during the early 1980s, had little to do with reality. In fact, Chrysler executives now concede privately that the success of Japanese auto makers in the U.S. market had an eminently scrutable cause: The Japanese were making a better car, and they were pricing it fairly. Public complaints about unfair practices notwithstanding, the real reasons for Japanese success had a major effect on Chrysler's strategy and decision making.

Chrysler was not alone, of course. The entire U.S. auto industry had to reshape itself. However, Chrysler's response to the challenge is especially interesting. Of all the major U.S. auto makers, Chrysler is most dependent on the North American market. Although producing and selling almost exclusively in North America, Chrysler found itself confronted with a competitive risk that involved, among other factors, currency differentials. The Japanese cost advantage was not solely attributable to currency, nor were Chrysler's strategic decisions. However, currency was part of the equation. Chrysler attempted to evaluate the competitive factors fueling Japan's successful drive for market share, and currency risk management fit into the company's mix of strategic and operating responses to that drive.

Chrysler used to have extensive overseas operations. As part of restructurings in the late 1970s and early 1980s, it sold off European, Latin American, and Australian investments. Instead of pursuing a global strategy, the company chose to concentrate on the North American market. The main factor in this decision was Chrysler's weak financial situation. There were only enough resources to focus on one market.

Chrysler's financial woes in the late 1970s coincided with three environmental shocks. On the regulatory front, the Corporate Average Fuel Economy Act (CAFE) required North American auto makers to increase the average fuel economy of their cars. CAFE set targets and timetables for the 1978–1985 period. At the same time, the North American automobile buyer began to demand smaller, fuel-efficient cars. The North American market had historically preferred large, powerful gas guzzlers, but oil prices had climbed up to shocking levels during the 1970s, and buyers reacted by tightening their belts. As a result, the American automobile buyer began to resemble his counterpart in the rest of the world. This shift in consumer preferences favored the Japanese manufacturers.

According to Chrysler Assistant Treasurer Hank Spellman:

> It's fair to say that the Japanese manufacturers, starting from a very small base in the late 1950s and early 1960s, had learned how to do it better than anyone in the world. They were primarily concentrated in the lower end of the market because that was the base of their domestic market, but they began to evolve up into the subcompact and compact segments of the U.S. markets with some pretty damn fine products.

At a time when the North American industry was just beginning to try to make smaller and more fuel-efficient cars, the Japanese had already mastered the art. Says Spellman:

If you begin to explore the factors for the Japanese success, some people attribute it to currency, some to productivity, some to better management. The reality is they were more efficient producers of higher-quality product more in demand in the North American market. People have the impression that they came in and under-priced the U.S. market, but I don't think that's a fair statement. The Japanese from a pricing point of view did not come in and try to viciously underprice the North American producers. They didn't have to.

Currency and Japanese Competition

Spellman ran Chrysler's competitive analysis team from 1983 through 1986. This team examined financial statements of Chrysler's competitors in order to calculate the competition's cost structure and to discover competitive strengths and vulnerabilities that might help shape Chrysler's strategy. "The objective of the analysis was trying to identify what was the Japanese cost advantage. How much cheaper or more expensively could they deliver a product to the North American market than we could?" he says. Spellman discovered that Japanese manufacturers not only had more and higher-quality fuel-efficient vehicles ready for delivery to this surging new demand in the United States but they were also able to price them just as the North American producers priced North American cars. In other words, the Japanese did not need to dump. Rather, since they were able to produce cars at the most cost-efficient level, Japanese car makers were able to make some attractive profits in the North American market.

Spellman's team ran numerous studies in an attempt to define the cause for Japan's cost advantage. It was at best difficult to break out what proportion of Japan's advantage came from a more efficient management system, what proportion derived from labor cost differentials, and what proportion from currency risk.

Currency was a factor. But how much of a factor? A move in

exchange rates had different, somewhat contradictory effects on Japanese costs. For example, about 20 percent of the cost of an automobile is raw materials. Prices for items such as aluminum, iron ore, petroleum, and copper are uniform worldwide and are usually expressed in dollars. So the Japanese manufacturers incurred some dollar costs even when their factories were all in Japan. Other dollar costs come when Japanese manufacturers ship cars to North America: The cost of ocean freight may have a large dollar component, depending on the shipping line used and the role of fuel prices in ocean freight rates; the cost of U.S. inland transportation, advertising, distribution, and sales support is also a dollar number. After allowing for these dollar costs, Chrysler's competitive analysis team calculated that about 60 percent of the total cost of a Japanese vehicle sold in the North American market was actually yen cost, Spellman says. Therefore, about 60 percent of the cost of a Japanese automobile in the North American market would be subject to change on the basis of currency moves alone.

This analysis further showed that the Japanese manufacturers had a cost advantage somewhere in the neighborhood of $2,000 per unit. In addition, they were making on average $2,000 per vehicle more than Chrysler on a vehicle sale in the North American market. To be sure, there were differences among the various Japanese competitors as well. Some were more efficient than others; some did better, and some did worse. But on the whole, with a cost advantage of $2,000 per vehicle, the Japanese auto companies had considerable flexibility.

They did not merely pocket the profit, or distribute it to shareholders. Spellman recalls:

> They were having a tremendous market share fight in their home market, plus they were in the process of expanding their penetration into the European market, and the sort of conclusion we came to is that they were using the profitability of the North American market in a period of export restraints to subsidize a vicious market

share fight in their home market and to subsidize to a certain extent their attack on the European market.

It is undeniable, then, that Japanese manufacturers enjoyed a substantial edge. Because of superior management, because of more efficient production methods, because they had the right product at the right time, and because the currency exchange rates were in their favor, they coined money. In the early 1980s, Chrysler analysts estimated that over 80 percent of the profits of Japanese auto makers derived from the U.S. market. A stronger yen would have diminished that competitive advantage, but it would not have eliminated the profits of the Japanese car industry. Says Spellman:

> It's interesting to note that if the yen gets strong, cars become cheaper to produce for the Japanese market because 20 percent of their costs, raw material cost, is now less in yen terms. Right now [July 1989] the yen is strong, and they're making money like bandits in the Japanese market.

Although Chrysler may have been unable to quantify precisely the impact of yen-dollar exchange rate shifts on Japanese competitors, the overall effect of their cost advantage during the early 1980s was clear. Besides subsidizing price wars in Japan and marketing campaigns in Europe, the Japanese plowed some of their profits into establishing production beachheads in the United States. Currency was certainly not the only consideration that led to approximately 2.6 million units of assembly capacity for Japanese cars in the United States, but it was a far from negligible factor.

Chrysler's competitive analysis of Japanese auto makers also took into account the fact that Japanese marketing success in North America was primarily in the lower end of the market: compact and subcompact cars. It was clear that if the yen were to appreciate, Japanese manufacturers would sacrifice much of their cost advantage in producing this grade of car for the North American market. Since about 60 percent of the cost of a Japanese car in the U.S.

market was yen-based, a stronger yen would put margin pressure on Japanese producers. This margin pressure might be handled in two ways. On the one hand, Japanese manufacturers could diversify their supply sources. On the other hand, they could move upscale, selling higher-priced, richer-margin vehicles. With hindsight, it is clear that Japanese manufacturers have done both.

In 1984, though, it was merely probable. With the yen well above 200 to the dollar and climbing, it became clear that Chrysler could no longer produce small cars competitively in North America. But Chrysler was in a quandary. For Chrysler's financial woes in the late 1970s had forced the company to put all of its eggs in one basket: small cars for the North American market. Of course, at that time, oil prices were high, and the North American consumer demonstrated a preference for small cars. Furthermore, government regulations, and in particular government oversight of Chrysler, required a focus on smaller vehicles. But most important, Chrysler only had the financial resources to make one bet. Management had decided from the perspective of bankruptcy that everything Chrysler built would use a 2.2-liter, four-cylinder engine, fuel-injected and highly efficient.

But by 1984 the dollar had rocketed and oil prices had fallen. U.S. automobile buyers had begun to change their product preference again. They were already forgetting the high gas prices of the 1970s. They wanted big cars. Chrysler's major domestic competitors, Ford and General Motors, had not suffered from Chrysler's financial constraints. They had, off the shelf, a mix of both big and small engines. Chrysler only had one engine, that little four-cylinder engine, so it needed a six-cylinder engine desperately.

The change in consumer preferences coincided with a shift in Chrysler's product strategy, which to some extent was determined by the yen-dollar relationship. With the yen at 240 to the dollar, and the Japanese car makers enjoying substantial cost advantages, Chrysler decided that it could not economically produce, in North America, cars for the low end of the market. Management decided to focus North American production on upscale, higher-margin cars, to rely on offshore sourcing for the low end of the market, and to look to overseas suppliers for components.

Currencies and Purchasing

In order to meet the immediate market requirements, though, Chrysler needed large engines immediately. At the time, large V-6 engines were only available from two suppliers. Both were Japanese. One of the suppliers would have required Chrysler to invest in some production facilities in North America. The other was willing to sell without such conditions. Chrysler was not in a strong bargaining position. It chose as supplier Mitsubishi Motors Corporation (MMC). This transaction was the genesis of Chrysler's foreign currency exposure management system. Spellman says that even today, the MMC engine contract accounts for nearly all of Chrysler's transactional foreign currency exposure.

Those negotiations took place in 1983 and 1984, when the dollar was surging toward its peak of strength. Chrysler economists, judging from economic fundamentals, had forecast that a dollar plunge was inevitable. However, management was far more concerned with getting the engines than with quibbling over currency clauses in the purchasing contract with MMC. In the first place, the yen had been weak for a long time. In the second place, Chrysler couldn't do much about it in terms of bargaining. They couldn't very well take their business elsewhere. For practical purposes, there was no elsewhere to take it.

The arrangement proposed by MMC, therefore, was as follows: From 240 to 220 yen per dollar, MMC would absorb the entire cost effect of a currency exchange rate shift. If the exchange rate moved within a band between 220 and 190, Chrysler and MMC would split the price effect fifty-fifty. From 190 to 130, Chrysler would bear 75 percent of the risk, and below that rate Chrysler would take the whole impact.

This contract, in other words, forced Chrysler to absorb nearly all of the dollar cost effect of a strengthening yen below 190 yen per dollar. From MMC's perspective, it was very favorable. After all, a strengthening yen usually means headaches for a Japanese exporter. But this contract guaranteed that more than half of the headaches would go to the buyer. Chrysler chose to give up some of the advantage it would otherwise have gained from a weakening dollar because Chrysler needed the engines. The decision was not an easy one, though, and seems to have generated some heated discussion. The story of how a senior Chrysler executive overruled his economics department forecast may be apocryphal, but it is eloquent: "Change your goddam forecast!" he said, "I'm going to tell you your forecast right now! The yen will be 240 forever, as far as the eye can see. . . ."

However, the exchange rate did not remain at 240 forever. In fact, it began to change shortly after the contract was signed. Since Chrysler pays for almost all of its purchases in dollars, it had to come up with many more dollars to pay for the engines. Ordinarily, it would be the Japanese supplier who moaned when the yen strengthened. But thanks to the contract, it was Chrysler that faced margin pressure. Competitive factors precluded Chrysler from simply passing on the cost increases in the form of higher prices. Yet from 1985 to 1989, the cost of the Mitsubishi engines increased by 39 percent.

"It hurt," says Spellman, "But it didn't hurt as much as it looked like. At one point, we were out two years hedging and saved ourselves a ton of money." The money saved through hedging mitigated the absolute increase in price on the engines. Chrysler's hedging program therefore helped ease the implementation of an overall strategic response to an economic risk. Shortly after signing the MMC contract, Chrysler management decided to manufacture a V-6 engine internally. The decision was made in part because of currency considerations—the falling dollar made MMC a very expensive source in the long run—and in part because Chrysler would be somewhat at risk if it depended solely on one outside supplier.

Chrysler's strategic response had to take into account not only currency but other environmental and competitive factors. Yet

Chrysler's tactical response was directed specifically at currencies. Until Chrysler's own engine production came onstream, a hedging program would provide some protection against margin erosion due to strengthening yen.

Forecasting

Since Chrysler's costs are to a large extent driven by the prices it pays for components (in fact, assembly labor in the U.S. auto industry only accounts for about 17 percent of the retail price of a vehicle), exchange rates are considered at the earliest stage of a purchase decision. Senior International Economist Robert Lippens says:

> We produce forecasts that go out ten years, and we try to influence people over in purchasing to get up to speed on what exchange rates are. We have a foreign source guideline committee which I've belonged to for the last couple of years, and we essentially write papers to try to help the people in purchasing to make decisions on the basis of what's happening now and what we forecast may happen in the next six months to a year. On the other side of the issue is international operations and they're trying to minimize exchange rate risk by developing joint ventures and building plants. And they're responding to our medium- and long-term outlooks as well.

Lippens forecasts long-term exchange rates on the basis of economic fundamentals: trade and current account balances, money supply growth, relative international pricing, relative income growth, interest rates differentials, productivity growth, and other factors.

The forecasts prepared by Chrysler's economists are disseminated to about one hundred decision makers in the corporation whose decisions may be influenced by currency values. Only one forecast is distributed; this is the official Chrysler forecast, and it is treated as if it were certain to occur. Decisions are made based on this forecast. Says Lippens:

> It's very difficult to adopt any other approach because there's so much machinery that gets set in motion when you give people alternatives. If you say that this exchange rate is only a mean forecast, merely the most probable, whether you are looking at something like the decision tree or at something like probability distribution forecasts around some mean forecast, you can't push the other forecasts that are part of that probability distribution through any part of the system with any accuracy.

At the operating level, administrative complexity precludes variable scenario analysis of exchange rates, Lippens says. For example, he explains, if he forecast rates as he might see them, with a 50 percent probability of one outcome but with a 25 percent probability of other outcomes either higher or lower, and distributed a forecast consisting of three distinct scenarios to the international marketing people, the purchasing people, and the hedging committee, it would create problems.

> It would be very difficult to make the outcome symmetric, in the sense that procurement and supply may like the 25 percent outcome on the left side of the probability distribution, international may like the 25 percent on the right side of the distribution, and nobody may like the mean. So where would we go from there? Do we force people to run three scenarios through the corporation, the mean and either side? It may be somewhat naïve to think that large corporations can generate that much paper work and actually make rational decisions on that basis.

At the top level of the corporation, however, possible variations from Lippens' currency assumptions are taken into consideration.

Spellman explains, "You have to do your scenario analysis at the top level, contingency analysis on variable assumptions like industry volume, market share, shocks to the system." Underscoring the link between currency rate shifts and Chrysler's market share, he elaborates, "I don't think we've ever done a currency shock scenario, because we would think that market share tends to show currency shocks better."

By taking the mean forecast, Lippens says, "you at least get a picture of what's going on." This mean forecast enters into the purchasing decision through a sensitivity analysis of foreign vendors' prices. Chrysler's purchasing covers a wide range of inputs, from vastly capital-intensive systems that require long-term supplier-buyer relationships to (literally) nuts and bolts that may be purchased opportunistically on the basis of price.

Van Jolissaint is responsible for forecasting the effect of exchange rates to purchasing's bottom line. Chrysler buys about $14 billion annually in North America, not counting about $3 billion in spare parts and Mexican sourcing. Chrysler has about $1.3 to $1.4 billion in currency exposure from sourcing out of North America. About two thirds of that is accounted for by the MMC contract, and the remainder, just under $500 million, is European curency exposure. Says Jolissaint:

> I give every month an exposure report that shows by major part number or part number grouping what we're buying from whom in the world and we (based on Bob's forecast) inform senior management what it's going to do to the checks we write during the year, on this material that we purchase overseas. And we also give buyers guidance when they are attempting to place business.

The auto industry is a long-cycle business. From inception of a new model to its presence on dealer lots takes about five years for most of the North American auto makers. Says Jolissaint:

> About two years before a launch, the buyer will actually be placing purchase orders or attempting to go out and

obtain quotes from all possible sources on the parts that we're actually going to be using on that vehicle that's going to hit the street. The parts' lifetime will on average be five years. So the buyer is interested in a time horizon that's from two to seven years out.

The long time horizon means it is critical for Chrysler buyers to recognize that exchange rates move, and that the moves will inevitably affect costs. Jolissaint explains:

> When you are out receiving quotes, no sane businessman will guarantee you a price forever. They'll quote a dollar price based on the exchange rates at time of quote. The most prevalent arrangement is that we will share the risk with the supplier up and down on a fifty-fifty basis from that time of quote, and the bigger suppliers that have a larger bureaucracy or are more administratively attuned will come in before they build the first part so that when they ship job one (it might be two years from now) they'll get paid the proper amount when they invoice us for the very first part that's shipped.

Chrysler expects its purchasing officers to make their buying decisions on the basis of fundamental competitiveness. Therefore, when vendors are invited to quote on new business, Chrysler buyers give the vendors a copy of Chrysler's exchange rate forecast. Chrysler tells the vendors to prepare their quotations in U.S. dollars on the basis of the Chrysler exchange rate forecast. Says Jolissaint, "The deal's not always won on price, but, to the extent that he can, he wants to get the prices on a comparable basis. All their quotes will be in dollars, and they will all be explicit, that it's based on assuming this exchange rate."

Says Lippens, "We have set up the committee which attempts to educate the acutal hands-on purchasers as to what foreign exchange issues are involved in making a buy." There are other issues, besides foreign exchange and economic competitiveness, that will influence a foreign sourcing decision. Jolissaint recapitulates:

> We care about a lot of things when we're making a sourcing decision: transportation, the ability of the supplier to give us parts that meet our quality specifications, and enough political stability that we can be absolutely assured that we will continue to get parts; and then given that, we feel certain that we're going to get the parts and the parts are of sufficient quality to meet our need, and the company's got internally enough R&D capability that we think they can keep current with technology. Then the last factor is price, and the exchange rate heavily influences the price competitiveness of going offshore rather than buying in the United States.
>
> There are lots of places in the world, including dirt floor factories in Mexico and Asia where you can make some hot metal stampings and castings, and we'll move there on the basis of just targets of opportunity, what we think the exchange rate is going to be, where we think it's going to be cheapest to do it. If there are tools involved we can move them fast. But if you're going into any kind of complicated assembly that will be time-consuming to move, it's different. If it's a little cheap die casting, I can probably move it in a month, but if it's a transmission, it may take me two or three years to move it, so what's the cost of being disastrously wrong? If the cost of being wrong is high, I think we'll tend to go with purchasing power parity, sharing of the shifts.

In general, Chrysler aims to share the opportunity and the threat of exchange rate shifts with suppliers. In order to negotiate the agreement, Chrysler buyers are directed to obtain a breakdown of costs and to exclude U.S. dollar costs from the sharing agreement. For example, ocean freight, U.S. distribution costs, duty, marketing expenses, and various raw material or overhead costs that the vendor pays in U.S. dollars may not change if exchange rates move. Only foreign currency costs are to be included in the sharing agreement.

Hedging Purchasing Exposures

When the buyer places a big new chunk of business, Jolissaint reports it to the individual responsible for implementing the decisions of the Chrysler hedging committee. He reports the details of the sharing agreement, and Chrysler's share of the exchange rate shifts will be added to the calculation of Chrysler's exposure. For example, if the vendor is Japanese and if Chrysler has agreed to share fifty-fifty the effect of dollar-yen exchange rate shifts on the yen price realized by the vendor, half of the yen costs in the contract will be added to Chrysler's yen exposure.

Although the purchase is denominated in U.S. dollars, the purchase contract has a clause saying that Chrysler will absorb a portion of the exchange rate threat or opportunity to the yen revenues of the vendor. In effect, Chrysler is responsible for paying a yen price on half of the purchase because Chrysler absorbs half of the currency impact. Thus, although Chrysler writes its check in dollars, the transaction exposure to a change in the dollar-yen rate exists just as truly as if Chrysler were purchasing yen from a bank and paying its bills dirrectly in yen. Therefore, a hedging program is in place to manage this risk.

Hedge Committee

Chrysler manages its hedging program with the help of a committee. As Spellman explains:

> The purpose of the hedging committee is to provide a
> forum, where we can all sit and discuss the factors that

are affecting currencies and what our individual opinions are about those currencies. It's got a couple of outside economists and investment bankers on it—we've got our inside economists, it's got people from our Washington office who always provide interesting insights. You get the economists talking about where things should be theoretically, you get the political people talking, it doesn't always match up. Out of that we make tactical recommendations: Do we want to extend or shorten certain coverage on currencies, or do we want to go naked, or what do we want to do?

Once a month, this hedging committee meets to consider Chrysler's exposure. The committee makes consensus decisions on whether, how, and when to hedge various exposures. As many as thirteen people may attend committee meetings to discuss and help decide on how exposures should be managed. After the monthly meeting has occurred and a consensus decision has been arrived at, the decision is implemented by treasury officers, who manage currency in addition to their other responsibilities.

Options

Chrysler has historically used forwards for most of its hedging needs, although in late 1988, the company began to use options as well. Options are useful when the direction of currency rates is uncertain. Formerly, when Chrysler was certain that the dollar would weaken, the company bought foreign currency forward. It was certain that the foreign currency would become more expensive in dollar terms over time, so it locked in favorable prices by using forwards. However, after the direction of rates became less clear, Chrysler began to use options. Then, if the dollar did weaken, the company would be protected, while if the dollar happened to strengthen, Chrysler would not have locked itself in to an unfavorable forward rate. Spellman explains:

From 1986 through 1987, and the first part of 1988, we were all tremendous dollar bears, and we used forwards rather than options. Now the consensus of the committee is not as strongly bearish as it was, it's not so clear that the risk/reward is so one-sided, and that's where you use options.

Mike Viola is the treasury manager in charge of Chrysler's trading room. He says:

It's a pretty conservative strategy in that we just buy according to our needs and we really just hedge our net exposure. If we have receivables and payables on the same currency, we just net the two, determine what our net exposure is—either an asset or a liability—and then hedge that accordingly, versus doing a gross basis hedging of receivables and letting a liability run naked, something like that. And then our hedging techniques are basically to buy; we're usually in a liability position and so we buy the currency forward.

Viola recounts a recent use of options for managing a yen exposure:

As a matter of fact we recently decided that instead of buying yen forward with forward contracts, we can buy them forward with a yen call option. That's all new to the group. We usually just stuck with the forward contract, but as far as a significant option strategy using range forward yens, or, they come in all names, mini-maxes, collars, whatever you want to call them, to cover yourself within a range by buying and selling options, either selling puts and buying calls, that type of thing, we haven't gotten into that and it would be a long educational process I think (for management) to convince them that this isn't really speculative and that it might be something to consider.

Managing the Trading Function

Viola manages a staff of two traders. This three-person unit not only handles implementation of currency hedging policies endorsed by the hedge committee but is responsible for precious metal trading and for various special studies and projects that have nothing to do with foreign exchange. Chrysler assigns people to the trading positions from other areas of treasury. The company does not hire professional traders, and the Chrysler staffers assigned to the trading unit are not encouraged to think of a career trading foreign exchange for Chrysler. Management of the hedge position is rather passive and consists of implementing the decisions and policies endorsed by the hedge committee. Traders are not measured on the basis of their success in making money on the position. Indeed, trading is only one of their responsibilities. As Spellman explains:

> We generally have a one-year training rotation through-out the company, but if a guy is in a trading position, we keep him there for eighteen months. People may come out of different areas, spend eighteen months, and go on to different jobs. If you keep professionals you lose them; they can make more money working for a bank. Of the eight traders we've had in that position, we've lost three of them outside. So we rotate our people through on an eighteen-month assignment. A person comes in and spends six months learning the administrative, the jargon, so when they answer the phone they can trade.

Natural Hedges

Exchange rates do not affect only existing transactions, however. They also affect long-term sourcing decisions. For example, Chrysler used to have a purchasing office in Brazil, but the company closed it because Chrysler sees the Brazilian crusado as overvalued. Says Jolissaint, "We just closed the office; we have no desire to purchase anything out of Brazil. We've moved everything we could move out of West Germany and Switzerland. We had significant buying, certainly in West Germany, and we have re-sourced everything we can get out." Chrysler used to purchase brakes from a European supplier, but Jolissaint observes that because of economic and exchange rate trends, Chrysler has moved that business back to North America. "Most of the re-sourcing that I'm familiar with," he says, "has been from overseas back to North America."

Recall that in the early 1980s, when the dollar was strong, Chrysler had opted to increase international sourcing. The decline in the dollar forced management to reconsider that decision. Yet, Chrysler has brought much of its overseas buying back to North America, Jolissaint says.

> Internationally oriented companies I don't think act the same way they used to act, in the sense that I think they view exchange rates as extremely volatile over time, so they hedge their bets. I don't think we brought as much back as would be dictated by simply the change in exchange rates.

In other words, Chrysler's sourcing arrangements are subject to continual review and evaluation on the basis of price competitiveness. For large, complex parts, such as brake systems, whose technology is difficult and expensive, the decision to change sources is driven by long-term economic factors. For simple parts, such as the nuts and bolts and stampings mentioned earlier, the decision is driven by short-term cost considerations.

Decisions on where to manufacture are also made in the context of exchange rate forecasts, but exchange rates alone do not determine a manufacturing decision. For example, the decision to manufacture minivans in Canada was influenced by differential labor costs between the United States and Canada, especially by the fact that the Canadian government picks up the tab for health care costs. Exchange rates were merely one element in the mix. Currency is much likelier to influence what segment of the market will be served by which sourcing arrangements. Currently, Chrysler is working on a joint venture to expand its production and distribution capacity in Europe. Suppliers to this venture, which will have assembly operations in both Europe and North America, will likely be selected in part based on their ability to service both assembly operations on a "just in time" basis. By relying on a supplier who is diversified with respect to currency base, Chrysler will cut itself some slack when the dollar moves against the European Monetary System (EMS) currencies. Because the supplier will be somewhat protected from currency shifts, the protection will flow through to Chrysler's purchase prices. Also, the design and engineering work will similarly be spread over two markets.

As the world automotive industry becomes more international, with a proliferation of competitors and a breakdown of clear market barriers deriving from product preferences, Chrysler's long-term strategy is also adjusting. Part of that strategic adjustment involves structuring the company so that it will be positioned for future growth. That growth is expected to occur not in the developed world but in the Communist bloc and in the less-developed countries.

Chrysler is discussing a variety of strategic moves for extending the company's spread and reach in these markets. Many alternatives involve strategic alliances. Chrysler is particularly strong in North America, but not particularly strong in Europe or Asia. By cooperating with other auto makers who have strength in those markets, and who stand to gain from Chrysler's strength in the Western Hemisphere, Chrysler can reduce its vulnerability to economic risks in any single market or sourcing site.

Strategic Risk

Meanwhile, Chrysler is beginning to investigate the possibility of using financial instruments to hedge its long-term strategic risk. Spellman says:

Strategic hedging says that currency changes per se are not bad or good, it's how they impact my relative competitive position. A currency change may help or hurt me, but it may hurt or help my competition more or less. The essence of my problem is a relative competitive problem. We're starting to look at it. A lot of it depends on the final results, the costs and the benefits. I still look at hedging as a way to defer the impact of currency, not offset it. Let's say we expect the yen to go back to 200. That would make the Japanese tougher competitors. You could go out and hedge that financially. Let's say you hedge it for five years. Then what do you do in the sixth year? All you've done is defer the problem from time x to time y. You've got to compare the cost of doing that against your reaction.

The issue of using financial hedges to guard against such competitive or operating risks is not limited to currency risk at Chrysler. The company has looked at similar strategies to manage its operating exposure to interest rates and to guard against supply interruptions in certain precious metals that are necessary to the production of catalytic converters. Spellman relates:

We have debated in the past the fact one of the exposures an auto company is subject to is interest rates. If rates go up, people don't buy as many cars, so why not do some strategic hedging on interest rate futures? We decided not to do it. It was hard to describe benefits and to get people to concentrate on benefits as opposed to the cost. The costs are very definitive. The benefits are somewhat nebulous.

CHAPTER 6

Union Carbide:
Bang for Bucks

One of the first U.S. companies to view currency risk as a money-making opportunity, Union Carbide takes a currency trader's approach to risk management. That is, it manages its currency exposures to make money on them. The operating managers sell off their exposures to a currency risk management unit in the treasury, and this unit treats the exposures as an income-generating portfolio. Union Carbide is not alone in this approach. However, it is unusual. The story of how one of America's premier industrial companies undertook a strategy that some with less knowledge and experience might be tempted to describe as stepping into a casino contains lessons that ought not be ignored. Carbide's program is, by all accounts, an outstanding success.

Policy Issues

John Clerico is Union Carbide's treasurer and CFO. He joined Union Carbide as international assistant treasurer in 1982. One of his first assignments was to conduct a corporate study of the currency risk management function at Carbide. The objective of the study was to determine what the function should do, what level of risk it might take, and what authority it should have.

Although Carbide had a professional risk management program in place when Clerico began his study, there was no clearly defined policy governing creation and management of foreign currency exposures. Unsettled issues included whether authority to manage currency risk should be centralized or decentralized, who in the corporation ought to manage exposures, how gains and losses would be allocated among operating units and corporate departments, and how currency risk affected various businesses. Clerico's study aimed to define the Carbide philosophy, establish the Carbide policy, and install procedures to implement that policy with respect to currency risk management. "Union Carbide at that time had about twenty significant worldwide operating businesses," Clerico explains. "Exposures were being created all over the enterprise. We had almost a third of our revenues outside the United States. There were many cross-currency, cross-border exposures. It was complex."

Task Force

In order to define the currency risk exposures of these businesses, Carbide established a task force that included representatives of finance and operating units. The reason for this approach was twofold. On the one hand, operating units knew the business and had experienced the effect of currency shifts on costs and revenues. Organizational politics also made a joint finance-operating effort necessary. Clerico wanted to implement an income-generating portfolio approach to managing Carbide's exposures, but he could not go forward without cooperation from the operating units. He explains:

> We could have come in over the top from a treasury organization standpoint and said, "Here is the Union Carbide philosophy. We think exposures should be managed centrally so the operating units will provide information on their transactions to the central unit, and we'll manage our exposures." Or else you could do as we did and have business and financial people from all parts of the company involved in the process so that you have everybody who is generating exposures and who is running a business where there is currency risk in agreement that this kind of a philosophy is the right one for Union Carbide. If it is simply mandated by the CFO or the CEO, well I've been around large organizations long enough to know that you are going to have difficulty getting it implemented because people won't feel that they have in any way participated in the process.

Task Force Working Groups

The task force included around thirty people who were part of a large steering committee. Union Carbide then broke the issues down into subject units, and the thirty were divided into smaller working groups, usually of four or five people. For example, one working group studied the problem of managing currency risk in hyperinflationary environments in Latin America. Typically, in dealing with each of the subject units, one or two group members were given the responsibility for coming up with initial proposals, leading the discussion and analysis of the issues, and so on. Out of the thirty people on the full committee, a dozen were operating executives, people who ran businesses and were selected for their knowledge of the international export markets and for their business exposure to international competition. Another dozen members of the task force came out of various corporate staff departments. In order to identify any tax implications of currency risk and hedging approaches, tax people were involved in addition to purchasing staff, accounting staff, and the corporate financial staff—financial people from around the world who were selected because they had particular interest in or exposure to currency risk management. Clerico stresses that it was "across the spectrum, about equally broken up among business guys, other corporate staff units, and financial people."

Short-Term, Transactional Currency Risk

The task force found that currency risk in the short term, roughly one year, differed from business to business. "For example," says Clerico, "if you sell a product in a marketplace where if the dollar moves you have the ability to adjust your prices, clearly you don't have a currency risk. We found ourselves with few of those businesses and more of the kind where we really were at risk."

The task force also determined that currency risk was a risk that could be managed. As Clerico says:

> That by itself is a fairly significant conclusion. Many of our competitors felt that the market price contained the best information that was available about a currency's future at any moment in time, and that therefore you should either hedge nothing or hedge everything. A large number of companies continue to believe that. But we came to a somewhat different conclusion. Therefore, we concluded that a selective hedging strategy could be

successful. But it required investment in people and systems and other resources.

Centralized Risk Management

Because the professional expertise to manage currency risk was both costly and scarce, Union Carbide decided that centralized risk management would be most cost-effective. So the company put a system in place that concentrated currency risk management in three corporate centers: one at headquarters in Danbury, Connecticut, one in Europe, and one in Asia.

Union Carbide risk managers in those three centers buy operating exposures from the business units. A business unit that sells its short-term transactional exposures to the central management team locks in its profit margins. "They are then held harmless as to any future movements in the exchange rates," Clerico explains, "We take the risk on at that stage, and are responsible for gains and losses. We can cover the exposures ourselves and square our position or we can keep the positions under management and attempt to improve them."

Not all companies agree that centralizing exposure management activities is best. Another large chemical company that manages its exposures as aggressively as Carbide organizes the system on a decentralized basis. This company, which outlined its approach on condition of anonymity, has considerable depth of treasury expertise in a number of regional financial centers. The treasurer says, "If you put the responsibility down to the field, the interplay between business and financial is very beneficial. That is where the action—the interface—with customers is: the front line of the battlefield."

Currency risk management occurs in the context of the overall organization. An organization with decentralized financial management cannot reasonably adopt a centralized approach to currency risk management. Similarly, an organization with centralized financial management needs to centralize currency risk management as well. This is especially true when corporations elect to trade for profit. In order to manage the trading function, management must itself be knowledgeable about trading strategies, threats, and possibilities. If only one or a few people at the top-management level understand currency markets, then decentralization of a trade-for-profit program invites disaster. It is simply not possible to manage what one does not understand. However, in order to make currency risk management add value to purchasing, marketing, and production functions, there must be close communication among the currency management unit and the functional areas. Where these functions are organized on a decentralized basis, currency risk management should either be decentralized or, if centralized, kept in touch with and available to the functions. This may be achieved through reporting systems and internal educational programs to inform operating managers about currency risk management capabilities and by encouraging operating managers to take advantage of the corporation's currency risk management services.

Some companies—Allied Signal is one example—strike a balance of sorts between the two approaches. Allied Signal is a decentralized multinational corporation that is active in three broad industry groups. Although currency risk management is centralized in a headquarters unit, the mandate of this unit is to function as an internal bank. Representatives of the currency management team work with operating management to ensure that operating management understands the range of currency risk management instruments available and how each instrument might be used to solve operating problems. The decision about whether or not to use the instrument belongs to the operating unit. The risk is a risk to the operating unit's success, and the decision about how to manage the risk is therefore an operating decision. Once the decision is made, the currency risk management unit executes the necessary financial transactions to book the instrument selected. This approach effectively decentralizes the management of currency risk without multiplying the corporation's investment in systems and expertise. However, this is not a trade-for-profit approach.

Long-Term Strategic Risk

The kind of exposure treated in Carbide's earlier study was a short-term, transactional exposure. Clerico distinguishes this from longer-term, economic exposures:

> We were dealing more with what was likely to happen over the next few months. If the dollar weakens 10 percent against the yen in ten months, we can be reasonably sure about what that means to our ability to export to Japan. But if the currency is predicted to move 10 percent five years from now, we can't at all be sure what that impact will be on our ability to export to Japan. For a one-year period, we can be fairly confident of the supply-and-demand balance in the business. So we know there will be either short supply, oversupply, or supply-demand balance. Therefore, all other things equal, a change in the value of the dollar will have a fairly easily quantifiable impact on our ability to sell into the Asian markets. However, if you go much beyond that, you're into a much different exercise, because the whole competitive position of an industry can change in a five-year time horizon.

For Union Carbide, therefore, competitive risk management means looking at the long term. It means trying to determine how all of the factors that impact profit margin change when exchange rates move. A properly done study of competitive risk requires the context of the business strategic plan, Clerico says.

> You have to take apart the revenue and cost structure and determine which of those elements are subject to variation depending on currency movements and then determine your competitors' positions in the same circumstances, so that you not only know that a 10 percent

change in the currency affects your own bottom line in a particular way, but more importantly how it affects your relative competitive position in an industry. Then you try to determine your response. We are beginning to do that now, and we have done it on a smaller scale with some of our businesses.

Currency and Strategic Planning

The competitive risk analysis now underway at Carbide is an integral part of the business's strategic plan. The strategic plan is the source for information on such factors as how much manufacturing capacity is going to be added and where it is going to be added. The strategic plan also contains corporate forecasts for the macroeconomic environment. But, as Clerico notes:

> Our situation is more complex than that of the other two companies that we are aware of that have done similar studies. They are Kodak and Caterpillar. They have simple businesses—I don't mean simplistic but I mean simple to understand in terms of their competitive structure, and how currency works its way through their competitive position. In our carbon products business, for example, where we are in the process of doing this exercise, we can manufacture in nine different currencies. That is, we have manufacturing centers where the cost base is in nine different currencies, and many of our competitors are the same way. So trying to determine what your relative competitive position is likely to be given a change in exchange rates at any given moment in time in the future is much more complex than talking about Kodak competing with Fuji, who has the yen-based cost structure, and Kodak, which has the dollar-based cost structure and some European cost structure. Same thing with Caterpillar and their Japanese competi-

tors. Ours are much more complex, more multinational, and more difficult to come to grips with, but we are doing it.

Trading Currencies

Meanwhile, the Carbide risk management program established after Clerico's initial study concentrated on financial management of shorter-term exposures. "We are aggressively defensive," he explains. "Our first goal is to help our businesses protect their profit margins. They are selling in foreign currencies. We don't always cover those positions immediately. So there is some risk. We do that, frankly, to enhance profit margins." In other words, currency traders at Union Carbide actively and aggressively work to maximize profit opportunities from exchange rate movements.

Speculation

Some corporate managements shun such activities, characterizing them as speculation. Clerico's answer to this charge is succinct:

> I respond to that by saying that you as a management decided to speculate with your shareholder's money when you decided to deal in any way, shape, or form with a buyer whose currency isn't the same as yours or which exposes you to business risk in a foreign economic environment. To say "I'm going to do nothing" or "I'm going to hedge everything" is just as conscious a hedging decision—hopefully—as it is to hedge selectively. For example, some companies who have the dollar as their functional currency and therefore see the gains and losses from the currency come through their P&L—perhaps the CEO of that company doesn't like to have to explain to security analysts why last quarter they had an exchange

gain and this quarter they have an exchange loss. Never mind that it might be to the best interest of the shareholder ultimately, he doesn't like to explain it. Therefore, he directs his financial department to hedge everything so that he has no currency gain or loss in the P&L. I know that is the position at some companies, and I'm not going to be critical. All I'm going to say is that that is a very conscious decision that might be either right or wrong depending on the ultimate outcome. There may be a cost to that strategy that isn't apparent simply from what you see in the P&L. If you want to eliminate any foreign currency risk you should sell only in the United States, and only in dollars.

Communication With Operating Units

At Union Carbide, dialogue between financial people and operating people is quite frequent. Exporting divisions and purchasing units around the company have been educated to the realities of currency risk, and they want to have the flexibility to buy and sell either in their home currency or in a foreign currency. Clerico underscores the importance of this dialogue:

> We feel that that's not just ideal, but that's critical. You have to have communication as to when the exposures are going to be created, you have to have open lines of communication between business and corporate finance people who are managing the exposures. If we weren't a part of their planning process, if they created the exposures and we found out about them when we saw a receivable or a payable, then it would be very difficult to do the strategy that we do.

Treasury contributes to business planning at Union Carbide by, among other things, providing an outlook for currencies that business managers use as they lay their plans and develop their business strategies.

> More than just a forecast, it's analysis of what happens to the bottom line given a planned competitive change in the industry from oversupply to shortage of supply combined with a forecast of movement in the currency. We try not to have a strategic planning process specifically geared to an exchange rate forecast, because then if the exchange rate changes, your strategy turns out to be wrong. We try to plan with sensitivity to exchange rate changes. Everybody knows, including our operating guys, that if we could sit here today and forecast exchange rates for the next two or three years out, we probably would not be working for Union Carbide, we would be doing something else.

Therefore, Union Carbide risk managers are encouraged to take a view on the direction of rates, but they are expected to adjust that view very quickly according to conditions in the real world of the marketplace. The Union Carbide philosophy stresses that ability to manage exposures is much different from ability to make a forecast. Risk managers are taught that their ability to manage the exposures will depend on how quickly they can deal with changes in the environment. They must always be prepared to adjust their own strategies in the light of market developments.

Staffing

"Control has several elements," Clerico explains, "but the single most important thing is organizational philosophy."

> For example, I have decided that I don't want to have career foreign currency risk managers at Union Carbide. On the one hand, I don't want to compete with all of

the commercial banks and investment banks around the world for career foreign exchange people. But it also is in line with my organizational development philosophy. I want as many broad-gauged international financial managers as I can have, not just a capital markets guy or a currency manager. However, that has a control element to it. Somebody who is in that position for ten years, knows it completely inside and out, he tends to know it better than anybody else in the organization, and he can cover up things if he's inclined to do that. Whereas if a guy gets rotated out of his position every two or three years, that sort of thing can't happen. He's got someone following on who he knows will be following, and that has a control element to it. No one is going to be so comfortable in that position that he can develop a long-term pattern of coverup without someone coming on in a fairly near-term time horizon to replace him. That's one element.

Another element is that I put only my brightest, high-potential people in that group, and their careers at Union Carbide are not determined on the basis of how much money they make for Union Carbide in the currency risk area. Clearly we have high standards and we want to measure performance and measure it quantitatively. But if you asked the three professionals who are in the group whether their next job is dependent on how they do in currency risk management for the next three or four quarters, they would say no. I let them know that mistakes are going to be made, and if that means we take some losses as a way to eliminate a situation that could grow to be worse, we take the loss and get on with it. You have to create an environment in which people feel free to communicate when they make a mistake. The attitude that I take when we have losses and mistakes is: Let's recognize that anyone who is in this business has losses and mistakes. The key to this business is to have more gains than losses by some fairly significant magnitude. We at Carbide have always been in that net position, but along the way you make mistakes and have losses. We have a performance measurement system which is very much designed to encourage currency risk managers to do what is right at the end of the day.

In situations where there is not such a system, people have gotten themselves and their companies into serious trouble. Lufthansa's disastrous forward position in the U.S. dollar illustrated the consequences of sticking with a bad position. Clerico says:

I think that if when somebody takes a position to go short or long on a currency and it turns out to be wrong, there can be a constraint on admitting to a mistake. So initially they think, "I've got a temporary market setback, but my scenario is still going to come about, so I'll stay with my position." It gets worse, it gets to the point where they are afraid to take a loss because it highlights their own mistake, and ultimately a small loss turns into a medium-size loss turns into a big loss. Of course, we have a full array of traditional accounting, auditing, outside controls on this activity. But I would maintain that equally important is letting the people know that "I hired you because I wanted to develop you and I think I can develop you as a broad-gauge international financial manager. I want you to do a good job in currency risk along the way. But if there are mistakes and it results in losses, we understand that; that is not make-or-break as far as your career is concerned." A lot of the very bad situations that some banks and industrial companies get themselves into is because that kind of environment did not exist. Somebody thought, "If I have to tell my boss I just lost $6 million, I'm going to lose my job, and I just gotta try to find a way to avoid that." That's the managerial issue.

Controls

Communication with financial institutions is also important. Currency trading is something of an old-fashioned business. Deals are made over the telephone. Typically, a corporation designates an authorized trader, and a bank gives him a line of credit with which to trade. At any point in time, the trader can pick up a telephone, call the bank, and commit the corporation to the full extent of the line. After the trade is done, the trader sends a confirmation to the bank, and the bank sends a confirmation to the company. In some cases, this has resulted in traders making bad deals and companies making big losses.

Apollo

One such example was Apollo Computer, an independent company until it was acquired by Hewlett-Packard in May 1989. In 1982, Apollo was a small manufacturer with sales of under $18 million. By 1987, sales had exploded to over $500 million. International sales were a big part of the business. In 1987, 52 percent of total revenues for 1987 derived from sales to unaffiliated customers outside the United States. Billing in twenty currencies, the company decided to manage foreign exchange risk and hired a well-known trader from Shawmut Bank in Boston. But instead of curbing currency risk, his trades cost the company $6.5 million, or eighteen cents a share, in the third quarter of 1987. In his letter to shareholders that year, chairman and CEO Thomas A. Vanderslice said that "this one-time charge was the result of unauthorized foreign currency transactions by an employee that were concealed from company officials and executed in direct violation of official policies and procedures." Company spokespeople were quoted in published reports after the incident as saying, "What happened was a very clever circumvention of controls, procedures, etc. But, as usually happens, one day there was a slip."

Yet the real slip at Apollo seems to have been a slip at the top-management level. According to bankers and company sources quoted in articles published by the financial magazine *Intermarket* and the regional *Northeast International Business*, Apollo's trader had unusually broad authority with very little control. He was responsible not only for trading currency but also for monitoring his own trading performance. One banker said that Apollo's trader sent and received his own trade confirmations. In effect, the company gave a single trader responsibility for functions that other companies divide among different departments and control with management oversight. The trader used his authority to roll a large, losing deutschemark position forward over a period of months. Like a gambler on a losing streak, he kept increasing the size of his bet, confident that his luck would soon change and he would win big. But Lady Luck never smiled for him.

Similar problems have arisen at other companies. Clerico underscores that at Union Carbide, financial institutions with whom the company deals are brought into the control process.

> Communications with the financial institutions are very tight. For example, say somebody has put a position in place and they want to do what are called historical rate rollovers. Six months ago they decided to sell the yen forward at 120, and it began to strengthen, so rather than mark that to market and take the loss, they might want to have the financial institution continue to roll that position forward, month after month, quarter after quarter, in the hope that eventually their forecast will come true, and they'll be able to close the position out with no loss. That's dangerous. That's how big losses get generated. So all of the institutions that we do business with know that they can only do historical rate rollovers with my personal acknowledgment and agreement to it.

Audits

Formal controls also include spot audits. However, Union Carbide has given considerable thought to how audits must be conducted. Clerico explains:

> My group is audited several times a year. I ask the auditing group to send the same people in every time, because if you don't and you have a three-week audit of the currency function, most of the time it takes the auditing people all of three weeks to get up to speed. The currency function has a language all of its own, a set of procedures all of its own, and if you are a fresh auditor who has never done this before, it's tough to ferret out irregularities. There are also what I call soft controls.

Soft Controls

By *soft controls*, Clerico means paying attention and listening. "Showing that you are interested, that you want to hear about results, showing that you know something about it yourself is important," he says.

> Part of the problem in some other companies where losses have occurred is that the only people in the company who are really knowledgeable about currency risk are the people who are managing it. I have a regular system of communication with my group. I go down and talk to those people several times a week. I know what positions are being taken. I offer my views as to what we ought to be doing, and what we shouldn't be doing. There is very little in the way of major strategy or position taking in my group that I'm not involved with. What positions are above water, which are under water,

why, what are you doing about it? . . . Unless you have at least some people in senior management who know enough about currency risk management to walk in and ask the right questions and be able to sense the attitude, then you run the risk of having five or six currency people there who are sort of running their own shop, inside a much larger company, and the only way anybody really finds anything out about it is when there's a gain or loss on the accounting records—and that's very dangerous.

Options

Union Carbide's system of controls helps the company manage an active and innovative program of currency trading that relies heavily on option strategies. Says Clerico:

One of the first things I did when I came to Union Carbide was to start our first experiment with currency options. I asked our CFO for permission to do this. I told him that it would be limited to $250 thousand of option premiums, that we would do it for a nine-month period. Since then, we have evolved what I think is a pretty sophisticated use of options. But the only way you find that out is to get in and try them, experiment with them. Two-hundred-fifty thousand dollars of option premium doesn't sound like a lot of money and it isn't. But you don't have to spend a lot of money to determine whether or not the strategy works. You don't have to buy a $10 million option position to find out whether the strategy will work, you can buy a $100 thousand option position and spend only $5 thousand option premium to understand the products, how they are traded, how they are priced, how they work, and who exchanges what risk for what reward.

From that modest, tentative, and experimental beginning, Union Carbide has developed one of the most innovative and active currency option trading capabilities in the United States. Union Carbide risk managers do not only buy options from financial institutions to protect themselves against currency moves. They also sell options to financial institutions. The revenues they earn from the sale of options contribute to the earnings of the risk management group. The group is expected to turn in positive earnings to justify the investment in personnel and systems.

Performance Management

As mentioned earlier, Union Carbide purchases currency exposures from the operating business units, paying them what is called the *inception forward rate*. That guarantees the dollar profit margin of the operating unit, even if the revenues are in foreign currency, and protects the business unit against the threat of adverse currency moves. The inception forward rate is the rate available in the market at the time.

Now the exposure comes onto the books of the currency risk management unit. The risk manager knows that at some period in the future, he must deliver dollars to the business unit at the agreed-upon inception forward rate. Under the Carbide system, the inception forward rate is a performance benchmark. As Clerico observes, if the risk manager merely covers his own exposure in the forward market, at the same rate which he has agreed upon with the business unit, value added by the currency management team would be zero. "We haven't cost anything but we haven't generated anything. But, having made an investment in people and systems and other resources, I expect our group to generate positive earnings in order to justify that investment."

Therefore, the risk manager at Union Carbide must improve upon the inception forward rate. But the inception forward rate is only one performance benchmark. The Union Carbide risk manager is also measured against the closing spot rate—the market rate available on the day the operating business unit collects its dollars from the currency management unit at the agreed-upon inception forward rate.

Therefore, Union Carbide manages its currency risk group through a dual benchmark system. The second benchmark is very important because it requires the risk manager to manage the exposure from the day of its inception all the way to its maturity. If a risk manager has agreed to purchase yen from an operating business unit at a rate of 200 yen per dollar, and the yen has strengthened to 180 yen per dollar, he may improve upon the inception forward rate of 200 by selling the yen forward in the market at 180. However, suppose the yen keeps strengthening. Suppose that on the settlement date, the spot market rate is 140 yen per dollar. As one Union Carbide risk manager says, "If I lock it up with a forward but the yen kept strengthening and I could have sold it as a much stronger spot rate on the closing date, then I would have given up some of my money. So the closing spot is critical."

Graham Spiers, formerly department head for Union Carbide's currency and interest rate risk management unit, now a currency trader with Travelers Investment Management Company, refers to the performance numbers, the gains and losses generated by this system of measurement, as *blue dollars*. They are "blue" because they do not show up on accounting statements, yet they are nonetheless real dollars earned or lost to currency moves. Spiers estimates that during the years he headed Union Carbide's team, the currency portfolio under management consisted of about $350 million of normal transactional exposure. He says that in addition, in order to take advantage of the unit's trading skills, Carbide during that period funded between $150 million and $200 million of its ongoing U.S. dollar short-term debt requirements through various foreign currency loans that were eventually swapped into dollars at a profit and hedged when Carbide's view of the market showed the timing to be right. Spiers estimates that during the 1984–1987 period, blue-dollar profits on this approximately $500 million currency portfolio ranged from a low of $3 million in one year to a high of $25 million. "The full effect of what we did in currency was probably much higher," he osberves, since currency trading helped the company do its basic business more effectively in international markets.

Yet despite a clear and unmistakable effort to make money on exposures, and notwithstanding a management system designed to judge Carbide's traders by how much money they make, Clerico objects somewhat strenuously when outsiders refer to his risk management unit as a profit center:

> We don't operate as a profit center. This is a group whose results can be quantified and we do measure them quantitatively, so they do have a bottom line. But we exist at Union Carbide because our businesses are internationally oriented, and we try to compete in international export markets. I don't want to foster an attitude that this is a group separate from the rest of the company. I want businesses to feel very much that we are a part of their team, that we are here to help them make money. I find that if you try to set yourself up as a profit center, then the rest of the company feels that they have to negotiate with you. I very much don't want to do that; it's counter to my own philosophy of working with the businesses.

CHAPTER 7

Monsanto:
Locking In the Plan

Monsanto's approach to managing its foreign exchange risk demonstrates that it is not necessary to invest heavily in systems and personnel in order to take advantage, prudently and conservatively, of financial instruments. It is very much a middle-of-the-road approach. Monsanto does not ignore the impact of invisible economic risks, nor does the company look at the financial markets as a source of extraordinary gains. Monsanto's corporate treasury is not a profit center. Yet the treasury is also not isolated from the operating units. While executing traditional treasury functions of transactional exposure management, Monsanto's corporate foreign exchange risk manager nonetheless works quite closely with operating units, explaining how financial instruments can help them do their own jobs better.

Thus, Monsanto is one of the clearest examples of how currency hedging techniques can enter the toolbox of operating managers whose selling, sourcing, and expenditure plans may be put at risk by volatile currency exchange rate moves.

Nearly 40 percent of Monsanto's 1988 income came from customers in Europe, Canada, Latin America, and Asia. Globalization is a key strategic theme for this $8 billion multinational. Therefore, it is hardly surprising that hedging foreign currency revenues should have a long history here. Monsanto established a senior-level committee in the late 1970s to evaluate the effect of exchange rate shifts on the company's reported results. "It served as a type of a steering committee for where we should be in terms of hedging exposures and how we should manage what was going on in the market," says Dave Guthrie, Monsanto's manager of worldwide corporate foreign exchange risk. The committee had included senior financial and operating people, but eventually it was dissolved. By the early 1980s, Guthrie says, foreign exchange risk management at Monsanto was being handled through normal organizational channels, for the most part focused in the treasury office.

There's nothing unusual about that. Almost every major international corporation has in place some kind of program to control the effect of negative currency impacts on transactional exposures. However, Monsanto has gone further than most. At Monsanto, operating divisions also hedge their annual plans, locking in anticipated margins and providing cover for market and price initiatives that might otherwise drag down reported income statement results.

Options Strategy

Monsanto Agricultural Company, for example, used an option strategy to ensure that a planned price reduction in the British market would not erode earnings. The price reduction was announced in 1988, to be effective in 1989. "The pound, at the time, was fairly strong," says Jim Hirschfield, Manager of International Administration for Monsanto Agricultural Company. "But there were some fundamentals in the U.K. economy which didn't look good to us, and we didn't want to be vulnerable to a considerable shift in sterling relative to the dollar."

The price cut would boost sales volumes and profits, but not immediately. There would be a lag effect. In the short term, the only result of the price cut would be a reduction in sterling income. Therein lay the rub. Monsanto measures its operating managers on the basis of the dollar income they return to the corporation. With a possible weakening of the pound against the dollar, the sterling price cut would wreck performance results measured with a dollar yardstick. In pound terms, income would be down, and in dollar terms, the pounds received would be worth less.

In order to ensure that a weakening pound sterling could not impair reported income, Hirschfield says:

> We looked at various means to protect that income stream. We looked at our currency exposure, the revenue less the cost, that was the profit that we wanted to protect. We took an option. It was in the beginning of the year, January, and we took that option to cover the selling period for that product, which is June through September.

The cost of the option was $700 thousand.

Guthrie says there were two reasons why the company chose to spend the money up front on an option: "One, your hedging costs are known up front. Regardless of what happens down the road you're not going to see your costs going higher than that. Second, not being 100 percent sure of currency direction, we didn't want to be left out if the dollar should take a bounce." Monsanto Agricultural Company could have sold pound sterling forward. However, a forward would have locked it in to delivering pounds at the agreed rate. The option, while it carried an up-front cost, preserved the company's ability to profit from favorable moves and did not lock it in to delivering pounds that it may not have had if business plans turned out to be overly optimistic.

Another perspective comes from David O'Neal, Manager of Financial Analysis for Monsanto Chemical Company, a separate operating unit independent of the Agricultural Company, which also uses options to lock in anticipated margins on its annual plan.

> It's like an insurance payment. We look at it this way: We're paying 1.5 percent premiums to guarantee that we're going to do no worse than budget. It's money that we spent. We realize that; it's gone. But we could not be worse than budget now because we locked the sterling in just about at the budget rate.

The use of financial hedging tools to protect planned operating margins and budget performance is now standard procedure at Monsanto. Operating managers consider hedging instruments to be part of their regular tool kit, a technique as legitimate as any other operational measure.

These managers protect what they call *parity exposures*. "We're protecting our earnings stream," says O'Neal, "the translation of our foreign results back into our dollar earnings."

It hasn't always been that way, though.

Discovering Currency Risk

A worldwide producer and marketer of agricultural herbicides, including such well-known names as Roundup, Lasso, Avadex, and

Machete, Monsanto Agricultural Company derives over half of its net sales of crop chemicals from non-U.S. markets.

Most of Monsanto Agricultural Company's international growth has occurred since 1980. Hirschfield explains, "As we entered into the 1980s, we had a product which had more of an application on a global basis than others we had had previously. That was when we made a deliberate effort to market globally, and it had a significant impact in terms of building international results." It was a tough time to begin an aggressive international sales program. In fact, the soaring dollar not only crimped sales performance, it also led to inefficient spending decisions by this fledgling global business.

"In many countries as we came into that period we kept adjusting our pricing," Hirschfield recalls. "We could do that the first few years. But toward the 1984-1985 period, the effect came through on our marketplace." The price increases on Monsanto Agricultural products were outpacing local currency inflation rates. Farmers had to pay more for Monsanto's products, but they could not pass the cost increase on to their own customers. "If we price at the rate of local inflation, the farmer can understand that costs are going up, but if prices are going up at twice the rate, it becomes quite difficult for him," Hirschfield says. "We saw our volume slip away."

Distortion in Management Information

Because operating management was judged on dollar results, it looked as if it weren't doing a very good job. No one really understood why. "Some of it could be explained by saying that when a product is introduced to the market, after a period of excitement about it, sales level off. We saw some of that, but that didn't really explain it all," Hirschfield remembers.

In order to boost sales, and overcome what management thought to be a problem of insufficient effort, Monsanto threw money at the market. "Even though our spending was going up in local currency, in dollars it was very low," Hirschfield explains. "We were putting more effort into the marketing, our field sales efforts, our product development efforts; we had to increase our promotions." However, since the dollar was still climbing, and results were reported in dollars, the additional spending did not show up clearly in reported results. Operating management still seemed to be dragging its feet. "We were spending more, but because of the dollar strength, it looked like we hadn't grown at all," says Hirschfield. "So internally, a disproportionate amount of resource allocation went into the effort."

Finally, it became clear that the shift in currency values had not only affected market performance but had obscured the information flows. The dollar's strength was creating static in management's picture of events in the field. Only a reporting system that allowed management to measure sales and expenses in local currencies could reflect accurately the impact of pricing and expenditure decisions on the local market.

> We remained on a dollar basis for reporting, but for planning purposes we also looked at a local currency basis. We started to look at the local currency statement side by side with the dollar statement. Now we saw that there were two levels on which to manage. One was the local currency side, the operational side, what was best for that market, what could we do in terms of pricing or resources. On the other side, when we translated results into dollars, we wondered, could we manage that?

The Task Force

In order to answer that question, Monsanto put together a task force consisting of both operating and treasury personnel.

The task force began by defining the dimension of exposure in the overall corporation. Since most of Monsanto's international business comes from the Chemical and Agricultural Units, the three-man task force included a representative of each unit in addition to a treasury representative.

The first step was to collect exposure information from the field. Regional offices were requested to break down their sales and expenses by currency. The initial process was very low-tech, Hirschfield says:

> At that time, it was more of a manual accounting process with spreadsheets. We didn't want to try to take a big expensive effort right away. We didn't want to spend that kind of money if it wasn't needed. We first wanted to develop a good understanding of what information was available, put it together in a not too detailed manner but sufficient to give us the dimensions of our currency exposure.

The task force determined that Monsanto had substantial, heretofore unrecognized, exposure to exchange rate moves.

> We usually didn't worry too much about what the chemical side was doing, and they didn't worry too much about what we did. But when we put the two together and sat down on a corporate basis, it was a very significant exposure we had, for the current year and for the next several years. It revealed a need to do more than the traditional price actions we had taken.

Experiments in Hedging

Once the exposure had been identified, it remained to convince management that the exposure could be managed. The task force—which did not include senior management—met some resistance to its recommendation that financial instruments should be used to manage this "hidden risk." It proceeded slowly. Says Hirschfield:

> We tried to demonstrate that other companies were doing it, and we went through a hypothetical case. We said, "Let's look at the situation today, and come back in six months and see what would the result have been if we took these actions." We did that case study, and showed it to management and said, "Here. If we had done this, we would have been able to achieve a result that would have been more positive than if we had done nothing." They said, "OK, let's go on to the next one, the real time phase, and actually put something at stake." Now we got that go-ahead, and we went out and sold forward, and we were really successful. If I recall, we had a gain of somewhere close to $2 million. It was relatively small considering our exposure and what we do today."

For its experiment, Monsanto Agricultural Company chose the French franc exposure. The selection of this exposure for the first experimental hedge of future income was no accident, Hirschfield says. France was an important market, and the company had a reliable track record there.

> We could predict a little better what our sales would be for the year—particularly the pattern of sales. Most of the sales take place during the fourth quarter. That pattern has existed for a period of time, and we felt quite confident about our expectation in terms of future streams of sales and earnings.

Economic Hedging and the Planning Process

The successful outcome of this initial experiment led to currency risk management and economic hedging becoming an integral part of the annual planning process.

> Each year, when we go into our budget and our next-year planning, we also sit down and discuss what actions

we would take side by side in terms of protecting that
currency exposure. So at the beginning of each year, we
have a plan in place for what actions we might take
depending on circumstances occurring throughout the
year. I'd say today the financial instruments are maybe
one third to 40 percent of that equation, and maybe
about two thirds are the operational adjustments.

In other words, financial hedges help to smooth operating
performance by removing—temporarily—the risk of adverse shocks
from exchange rate volatility. They buttress the traditional operating
manager's repertoire of pricing, sourcing, and expense adjustments.

They complement the other techniques we use. We can
only use price to a certain point; we can only change our
sources to a certain point; if we want to change our
spending we have to think of certain things not only for
today but for the future. The foreign currency financial
instruments help to balance that out, they let us do fine-
tuning of that total management of exposure.

Operating Management

At Monsanto, the hedging of future income is an operating company decision, not a corporate decision. Area managers are evaluated on the basis of their dollar results, and the earnings or losses
from hedge contracts they have entered into also flow into their
performance appraisals. As a result, there is a relatively high degree
of awareness among Monsanto's operating management of the
advantages and disadvantages of currency hedge instruments. Some
of the techniques used by Monsanto operating divisions are quite
sophisticated.

Monsanto Chemical Company is the biggest of Monsanto's
five operating divisions, accounting for nearly half of the corporation's income. In 1988, Monsanto Chemical earned $486 million

on sales of almost $4 billion. Chemical has a longer international operating history than Agricultural, and Chemical's operating managers are correspondingly adept at exploiting currency advantages. Says O'Neal, "We've been doing that for years and years in Europe. When we sell to the Soviet Union, depending on how currencies are going, we may bill them in dollars, we may bill them in pounds, we may bill them in deutschemarks."

The effect of the sustained weakening in the dollar after 1985 helped the company's exports from the United States.

> We're like everyone else. It made us more competitive. We're not fine-tuned to say what happens with a one or 2 percent change in the dollar. But if we have a 10–20 percent change in the dollar, we have an idea of what that will do to us in our major products.

There are some businesses and some markets where currency values spell the difference between death and survival. "As an example, when the dollar was strong, we could not compete out in the Far East with acrylic fiber sales," O'Neal comments.

Proxy Hedging

Chemical does not trade currencies for profit. On the other hand, it is not averse to taking advantage of interesting opportunities to maximize hedging gains and minimize costs. Proxy hedging is one such technique. During the annual planning process, Chemical's regional offices report their expected sales and revenues by currency. O'Neal explains:

> We establish a budget parity rate. We say our budget is based upon these exchange rates. If we feel that the dollar is going to strengthen against those currencies, it means that they will translate back to fewer U.S. dollars. We're not so sure we want to take fewer U.S. dollars,

since we consolidate in dollar reporting. So we may go out in the market and hedge if it is cost-effective.

Naturally, when European currency exposures are measured, sales and costs denominated in U.S. dollars are excluded from the total.

> They identify their cost structures by currency. If they're buying raw materials in Belgium but they're buying them from a German company in deutschemarks, that is a deutschemark exposure—but their conversion costs in Belgium would be Belgian franc exposures. We also identify our MAT costs—marketing, administrative, and technical—by currency. Since our European headquarters is in Brussels, most of it is in Belgian francs, but we have sizable sales offices in Germany or Italy or France or the U.K. or wherever.

Sales forecasts are also analyzed by currency.

British pound sterling exposures go into a separate pool from continental European currencies. Monsanto Chemical excludes British pound sterling from its European exposure report because the pound sterling does not move in tandem with the currencies that form the EMS.

"We put all the rest together—" O'Neal says, "the deutschemark, the lira, the French franc, the Belgian franc—into one common net exposure. Then we do two separate hedging actions. We'll hedge the pound sterling side in pounds and we'll hedge the continental currencies in deutschemarks.

This approach, in which the German mark serves as a proxy for currencies with which it moves in tandem, allows Monsanto Chemical to take advantage of the greater liquidity of German financial markets. It can be expensive to hedge in Italian lira, Spanish peseta, or other European currencies whose financial markets are less liquid than Germany's. But since the EMS currencies move together in a band, it is possible to approximately hedge an Italian or Spanish or Belgian exposure by taking a position in German marks.

Chemical prefers to use options for hedging of future income, so long as the cost is reasonable. When the cost of options is not reasonable, some creativity is called for.

Hedge Gains Reduce Hedge Costs

During the 1989 planning process, which occurred in late 1988, it was decided to hedge European currency earnings. But there was a problem. Option cover was unacceptably expensive. O'Neal explains:

> At that time, the deutschemark had already depreciated to the dollar, and we were already sitting about 3 percent above our budgeted rates. They wanted something like— I think we were looking at a 2, 2.5 percent premium on top of the 3. We said, "Let's wait and see." But we did develop a policy at the time. We said if the deutschemark strengthens another 3 percent, we will go with some sort of hedging at that point in time.

In May 1989, that exchange rate hit the trigger point and it was time to hedge. "We looked at the forward area. We looked at the option costs, and they were very high," O'Neal says. In fact, the option would have given Monsanto the right to sell German marks for more money than they were then worth on the market.

> We don't generally like forwards, but it was the lower cost at this point in time. We took forwards out to cover the remainder of the year's exposure. Our timing was superb, because the dollar strengthened substantially over the next two weeks. We had substantial gains. We rehuddled. We have some downside risk now. If the dollar were to go into a tailspin and go back down, we

could lose money on it. You don't take risk when you're trying to protect your budget, so we said, "Why don't we spend some of the gains we've already got in our pocket and buy options going the other way to protect us on the downside?"

Monsanto Chemical, in other words, purchased options to protect the gains it had on the forward contracts. The forwards protected the company against a strengthening dollar, and the options protected it against a weakening dollar. "If it strengthens, we've got definite gains and our options are of no value," O'Neal says. "They're out of the money then, we've just paid a premium for protection. If it weakens, we have got options that will cover any hedging losses that we would have on the forward contracts."

Speculation vs. Management

Some people might view this type of activity as speculative. However, Hirschfield claims that "if you do nothing, then it's more speculative. Because then you are open to any event occurring. So in a way you are taking more risk. Without taking action, you're not protecting, you're still going to live with great uncertainty."

Monsanto puts the onus on operating management to regard currency shifts as manageable events. Budgets, once approved, must be met. The dollar budgets are drawn up with a particular exchange rate scenario in mind. If that scenario does not match the real world, it's no excuse to say that the exchange rates moved.

The evolution of currency risk management at Monsanto has been very much a bottom-up affair. The development of hedging strategies that lock in future income was driven initially not by a top-management fiat but by a recognition at the operating level that currencies were a part of everyday business in the global marketplace. A recent presentation to top management explained the use of currency hedging techniques as an adjunct to traditional operating measures used to cope with currency shifts. In the long term, currency differentials may merely reflect different rates of inflation between countries. However, in the short term, the volatility of exchange rates is a fact of operating life. A price increase, or a change in how and where a product is sourced, may not be desirable. This does not mean, however, that the brunt of sudden swings in currency values must batter the company's dollar earnings. Financial instruments allow management the flexibility to maintain optimum operating procedures regardless of short-term currency volatility.

Transactional Exposures

Monsanto differentiates between the economic exposures just discussed and transactional exposures. Monsanto's corporate transactional foreign exchange exposures average somewhat under $200 million, and this portfolio is managed by Guthrie, a seven-year veteran as manager of Worldwide Corporate foreign exchange risk.

Monsanto has two netting centers, one in Singapore and the other in Brussels. According to Guthrie:

> The netting is basically an efficient cash management technique if you've got funds flowing in a lot of different currencies. If somebody is paying you in one currency and you have to pay somebody else in that same currency, then by combining the two, you save conversion costs. Also, by centralizing everything, you can build up your transaction size so you can hedge cost-effectively.

Using software packages from outside vendors to analyze trends in exchange rates, Guthrie manages Monsanto's transactional exposures conservatively. "We're not trying to pick the tops and the bottoms of the market," he says. "We're trying to determine whether there are significant trends one way or another and be on the right side of those trends." His approach to managing the transactional exposures is quite cost-conscious. After all, the goal is to limit negative impacts to the dollar values of these exposures, not to maximize the dollar returns or to trade the exposure for profit. "For those types of exposures we're basically just using the forward contracts to hedge," he explains. "We can selectively hedge and we can move in and out of positions. Forwards are a good instrument in terms of doing that."

No Excuses

Monsanto's approach to currency risk management distinguishes two types of risk that are of concern to the corporation. The first type, the transactional, is a risk that is easy to identify and to manage. Transactional risk shows up on the balance sheet as a foreign currency receivable or payable. However, the second type of risk, the risk that currency shifts may frustrate operating plans and distort management's understanding of what happens in the field, is more evasive. Unmanaged, this hidden economic or parity risk can do far more damage to the corporation than most of the visible risks. Monsanto, having identified the types of risk, developed procedures to manage them. These procedures do not involve heavy investment in systems and personnel in order to add currency trading gains to the corporation's sources of income.

Instead, Monsanto has left to operating managers the decision about whether and how to address the risk posed to their business plans. They know that the tools are available, and they know how to use them.

They are responsible for using them, and they are responsible for not using them.

There are no excuses.

CHAPTER 8

Digital Equipment Corporation:
When the Dollar Is Still King

Unlike all of the other companies profiled in this book, Digital Equipment Corporation rejects the use of financial instruments as an adjunct to competitiveness or as a source of financial gain. In fact, Digital Equipment Corportion considers currency to be neither a competitive opportunity nor a competitive threat. Digital's approach to currency risk is to make it disappear by converting all revenues into dollars at forward rates prevailing when sales are certain. Options are considered dubious bets in this shop, and any attempt to maximize the value of foreign currency revenues in dollar terms is branded speculation.

While DEC's approach may seem a little old-

fashioned, the fact is that DEC's competitive environment has not yet delivered the kind of shock
that converted the other companies profiled in this
book to a more active, more innovative approach
to currency risk. Furthermore, DEC's story shows
us how organizational politics and management
structures figure in the development of a currency
risk management program. Examined here is the
evolution of one of the largest forward hedge portfolios in the world, a portfolio measured in billions,
and the development of a currency hedging system
that virtually disallows the exercise of human judgment with respect to currency risk management.

Digital Equipment Corporation (DEC) is a Yankee entrepre-
neurial legend and one of the world's most successful computer
manufacturers. Headquartered in Maynard, Massachusetts, DEC
competes head-to-head in most international markets with a company based not far away in Armonk, New York—IBM.

It is significant that DEC and IBM, as well as most of their
lesser competitors, are U.S. companies. From a currency risk
management perspective, it means that the dollar is the currency
that determines pricing in the computer market. Indeed, when the
dollar strengthens, computer prices expressed in local, nondollar
currencies tend to rise. When the dollar weakens, local currency
prices may remain stable or fall.

Dollar-Based Competitor

This is a very different situation from that faced by manufacturers
of heavy earth-moving equipment, automobiles, or many other
products where competition from Asian manufacturers is a fact of
life. The computer industry is still a U.S. dollar arena because U.S.
dollar-based companies dominate the market. As Japan continues

to develop as a competitor, this situation will certainly change. Eventually, the computer industry will look like most other industries, and it will not be so easy for U.S. dollar exchange rates to flow through into pricing.

In fact, some of DEC's competitors are already preparing for the day when the computer industry will experience what other industries have known—the competitive force of currency moves. But for now, the impact of currency moves on competition in the computer market is not a major consideration for DEC managers. If changes in the value of the dollar can be passed along to customers in the form of higher or lower local currency prices, the manufacturer has no currency risk. Competitive constraints do not usually preclude DEC from passing along changes in the dollar's value to customers.

This is not to say that currency moves are not important at all. DEC sells a lot of computers outside the United States, and prices are quoted in non-U.S. dollar currencies. For marketing reasons, the company wants to be perceived as a local company in every market where it sells. Thus, DEC wants to look like a German company to German customers, a British company to British customers, a Japanese company to Japanese customers. The local company image can be distorted if prices in local currencies rise and fall every time there is a move in the value of the dollar relative to the mark, the pound, and the yen. But DEC managers are measured on the basis of the dollar earnings that they return to this very Yankee company's Massachusetts headquarters. The dissonance between the goal of maintaining stable prices in local currencies and the goal of returning the most dollars possible to the company has helped to shape DEC's approach to currency risk management.

Conservative Approach

The company's approach is very conservative insofar as it protects reported earnings from sudden shocks. DEC hedges all of its foreign currency revenues. The hedging activity is centralized in corporate treasury. Operating managers are expected to manage their business the old-fashioned way: by cutting costs and/or raising prices when the dollar strengthens. Of course, operating responses are ultimately necessary for any manager confronting long-term shifts in currency values. After a while, hedges run out, and all managers have to face the music. At some companies, financial hedges enter the tool kit of the operating manager. But DEC does not accept the proposition that financial hedging instruments are useful adjuncts to an operating manager's business strategy. It centralizes all hedging activity in the treasury department, and protects accounting results by hedging all transactional exposures on the forward market. This approach locks in current forward rates. DEC does not consider options to be like insurance at all, and does not use them to hedge business plans or even transactional exposures. Rather, its treasury personnel associate options with speculation. DEC considers an option premium to be like a bet placed on the direction of currency rates. If currency rates do not move in the right direction, the option does not pay. For this reason, the word *speculation* comes up frequently when DEC financial people talk about currency options. An option trader is as out of place in DEC's treasury area as a croupier at a Baptist church picnic.

Protecting Accounting Results

DEC's hedging program exists to lock in dollar revenues with certainty. Because the company does not want operating managers to be severely penalized by very short term moves in exchange rates, the hedging program provides about six months of protection to forecast sales levels. There is a flip side to this protection: When the dollar weakens, operating managers get a share of hedge losses as well.

DEC treasury staff describe the company's philosophy of currency risk management as risk averse. *Risk*, for DEC, means risk to accounting results and reported earnings. DEC believes that currency risk can be eliminated if the company turns all foreign currency revenues into dollars immediately, at the forward rate. Given the competitive structure of the computer industry, the company has no fear of a change in the dollar-yen rate opening a big gap between its prices and the prices of a Japanese competitor. DEC's biggest competitor is IBM after all, and price is hardly ever the sole determining factor in the purchase of a computer system. Furthermore, because DEC considers the currency markets to be efficient, DEC believes that the forward rate includes all of the available information about the future direction of currencies so that the forward rate is a fair price and there is no point in trying to benefit from rate moves. With nothing to fear on the downside, and believing that there is nothing to gain on the upside, DEC considers currency management a straightforward matter of turning foreign currency receipts into dollars quickly.

Hedging Program

In terms of sheer volume, DEC's hedge portfolio is huge; it is measured in billions of dollars. Overseas operations account for over half of the company's sales, and the struggle to reconcile incongruent objectives and priorities with respect to currencies has caused DEC to visit and revisit the subject of currency exchange risk management several times over the course of the company's history. Not only currency values but management and strategic issues had to be taken into consideration as DEC developed its program.

Thomas Downing, Manager of Foreign Exchange at DEC, describes the DEC system as follows:

> We separate our hedging program into two pieces, the short-term piece for financial hedges, and the long-term piece in which we rely more on the operating managers to manage. The pressure is on them to return dollars to the corporation. They've really been faced with manag-

ing that exposure, by taking pricing action, shifting sources, reducing costs, and, ultimately, strategic actions such as changing the load of manufacturing plants, or the location of manufacturing plants. [In the very long run,] changes in currency reflect changes in inflation rate, so over the very long run the prices sort of naturally adjust.

In other words, if the French franc is weakening, in the short term the company is going to be squeezed. But in the long run, DEC relies on the theory of purchasing power parity, which says that inflation in France will accompany a weakening currency, so price increases necessary to maintain stable revenues in U.S. dollars will match the general direction and magnitude of franc prices on other goods as well. In the short run, though, the operating management is faced with a real problem. It takes time to make operating adjustments, but currencies change overnight, randomly, with no immediate short-term relationship to inflation.

Managerial-Political Issues

Marty Ford, formerly DEC's CFO for Europe, was based in Geneva during the early 1980s. He has since left the company. Reminiscing on his tenure as European finance manager for DEC, he recalls that DEC's prices used to be set out of corporate headquarters, in dollars, for all markets worldwide. This approach meant that local currency prices changed whenever the dollar moved.

They would literally beat up people to keep the dollar's worth of profit. We got to the size and got the independence in Europe to say, "Hey, this is crazy," jockeying our German customers around every time there's a move in currencies up or down. We'd be going all over the place. Our major competitor was IBM and they weren't doing it. They were maintaining the prices based on the

German market, not influenced by currency moves upward or downward. And that's the position we felt we
had to get to.

According to Ford, when DEC was establishing its risk management program, the fundamental point at issue was not how to
manage currency risk but how to manage the business. The alternatives were, on the one hand, to be a dollar-based company or,
on the other, to manage locally, which meant setting prices locally,
controlling costs in local currencies, and managing the local managers on an operating performance in the local currency, regardless
of where the dollar swung. Ford recalls:

> We were trying to move to that in Europe. The viewpoint
> needs to be a lot longer. When you get right down to it,
> the major issue we were really trying to work was getting
> balance in our currencies, to have production in Europe
> and to have development in Europe and so forth so that
> the net currency exposure was more balanced.

Natural Hedge

Of DEC's 130,000 employees, approximately 50,000 to 60,000 are
based overseas. Wages for these employees are a major portion of
DEC's natural hedge. To the extent that the dollar value of DEC's
international sales may rise or fall because of dollar weakness or
strength, the dollar value of this wage expense rises and falls as well.
DEC's overseas manufacturing plants also source overseas, which
means that a large portion of inventory costs are also foreign
currency costs and can therefore serve as a natural hedge.

For a company to be perfectly hedged by local currency
expenses, the expenses must be in the same currency as sales
revenues. A perfect natural hedge would mean, for example, that
all goods shipped to customers paying in francs would be manufactured in France using only materials paid for in French francs or

that all sales billed in Japanese yen would use only merchandise sourced from yen-based production centers and be put together by workers paid in yen. This is obviously impossible. DEC continues to strive for greater balance, but it cannot rely entirely on natural hedges.

One reason is the nature of the computer industry, an industry characterized by rapid changes in technology. Says Ford:

> Most people think of manufacturing as brick and mortar and so forth. Digital's businesses today have significantly changed. They don't need many manufacturing plants today. The technology has gone from where they used to have twenty or thirty chips on a board and ten boards in a computer to one board in a computer with one chip. So you've gone from two hours of direct labor down to literally five minutes or under. So the amount of direct investment in those kinds of materials is not there. So it's very, very difficult to get that balance without tremendous economies of scale. With the exception of IBM, I don't think anybody else in the industry has it.

Selective Hedging

DEC's international sales as a proportion of total sales have grown from 39 percent in 1980 to 56 percent in 1988. In part, this reflects the weakening of the dollar after 1985. But DEC has also grown internationally. When the company first began to sell internationally, it hedged selectively. Drawing on the advice of outside financial consultants to decide whether a particular foreign currency revenue stream or transaction was likely to gain or lose value in dollar terms, DEC's treasury sold forward a greater or lesser proportion of the exposure. In the late 1970s, when the dollar was weakening, DEC had hedged part of its foreign currency revenues, but it left part of them unhedged. The unhedged portion gained in value from the weakening of the dollar, and the partial hedge provided protection in case the dollar reversed its course and strengthened. When, in the early 1980s, the dollar began its steep climb, the unhedged portion of the portfolio rapidly lost value.

These losses were the catalyst for a change in DEC's approach to hedging. They got the attention of top management, and selective hedging was no longer considered to be acceptable. The big loss had convinced DEC senior management that any attempt to forecast and benefit from currency moves was sheer speculation. Management decided that DEC should hedge all flows.

This decision occurred in 1982.

Hedging and Performance Measurement

At first, DEC did not distribute hedge results to the operating units. But the company had a quarterly planning system that measured managers against a budget exchange rate so that they would not be penalized by currency shifts that were beyond their power to address. Otherwise, operating managers who were being measured on the dollar value of their sales would have looked bad when the dollar was strengthening. When the dollar is strengthening sales orders denominated in foreign currencies lose value between the time they are booked and the time the merchandise is shipped. After the merchandise has been received by the customer, and the order has become a receivable on DEC's books, the foreign currency receivable loses value in dollar terms until it is collected. DEC's performance measurement system initially established quarterly benchmark exchange rates against which managers were measured. Treasury had managed the actual exposures by selective hedging. But, in 1982, DEC had begun to hedge all of these orders in the corporate treasury area.

In 1984, DEC decided to abandon the quarterly budget rate approach to measuring performance and merely to include the hedge gains or losses results in the reported results of operating managers. The new approach required a very complicated internal accounting change, and it took a while to implement.

In 1985, the dollar peaked. Then, between 1985 and 1988, the dollar weakened precipitously. Operating managers might have enjoyed phenomenal windfall gains as their foreign currency sales were translated back into dollars. Orders from non-U.S. customers gained dollar value between the time they were booked and the time the merchandise was shipped, at which point the foreign currency receivables gained in dollar value between the time the customer was invoiced and the time he paid the bill. However, the currency gains did not flow through as a windfall into operating managers' results because DEC had decided to include hedge gains and losses in operating results. From 1985 to 1988 they were mostly hedge losses.

Going Without Hedging

Therefore the hedging program was making people unhappy. "We were throwing all of these losses into the operating results," Downing says. "After a while, people began to wonder if it was all worth it." In 1988, DEC took another look at its hedging system.

Ford remembers:

> At one point, the recommendation from one of the senior managers was to do away with hedging completely and just say, "Hey, let it roll the way it is." As long as we explain it to Wall Street, you know, they'll understand it. We're in this for the long term anyway, and it doesn't hurt the actual cash impact on us, we're not moving cash around that much.

However, analysis determined that doing away with hedging completely would expose the company to swings of from 20 to 25 percent in earnings prior to the end of a quarter. "Once everybody saw that," Ford says, "they said, 'no, we can't tolerate that.' "

Selective hedging had been abandoned in 1982. There was no gong back to a practice that DEC management considered to be speculative. The alternatives were simply to hedge all flows or to hedge none. Hedging none was unacceptable because of the volatility it would introduce into reported earnings. The 1988 study therefore concluded that a program of hedging all flows should continue, and it endorsed the status quo.

Short-Term Hedging

DEC's history and the development of its hedging program has led it in the direction of a comprehensive hedging program to address short-term currency exposures. Asked to define the currency risk management philosophy governing the hedging program, DEC treasury staff reply, "We define it as cash flow risk and it's the risk that we won't be able to take compensating action in the face of changes in exchange rates to maintain the desired level of cash flows." For DEC, cash flow means short-term reported U.S. dollar flows. The company manages its hedge program on the basis of optimizing accounting results.

The hedging program is intended to cover short-term exposure. Downing explains:

> Essentially we forecast our cash flows over six months. We distinguish between dollar cash flows and local currency cash flows. We do this subsidiary by subsidiary, which is in effect currency by currency. We calculate the sales we'll be making, the receivables we'll be collecting, local currency expenses, to get a net number which for the most part is a long exposure in most of our currencies. We pool all of the subsidiaries. We'll have a Japanese yen exposure from the Japanese subsidiary, but we'll also have yen exposure from other sources. All of DEC data collection gets to a central point for hedging. We then enter foward contracts.

DEC repeats this process of data collection monthly. The company maintains a rolling portfolio of hedge contracts, which is updated as contracts expire and exposures change.

Assistant Treasurer Paul Milbury explains:

> In our hedging, we don't do any speculating whatsoever. We collect the data, and then we hedge 100 percent of those exposures at all times. We're not trying to guess where the currencies are going. What we're interested in is getting certainty of those cash flows, or transactions, not trying to make money on them.

Using Forwards

DEC uses only forwards in its hedging program. When DEC sells its foreign currencies forward, it agrees to deliver foreign currency to the bank at some point in the future at the exchange rate prevailing today. The forward rate in an efficient market includes all information about the direction of rates, so it may be better or worse than today's spot rates. DEC believes that markets are efficient.

Opportunity vs. Risk

Of course, the chart of the U.S. dollar against a European currency over a six-month period can look like an Alpine range. DEC's rigid hedging program means that at times the company may receive many fewer dollars for its European currencies, and at other times may receive many more dollars. Indeed, the rigor of DEC's transaction hedging program—all foreign currency exposures must be sold forward, and the forwards must be booked within a few days of the monthly exposure report—means that DEC's currency trader sells foreign currencies regardless of whether, in his judgment, market trends and economic data seem to indicate that these currencies are gaining in value. A day or a week of waiting may add considerable dollar value to the flows, but waiting also adds risk. An option may ensure that the flows cannot lose value, while retaining the upside potential—if the trader's judgment is correct. But such positions may cost money, and that money will be at risk. DEC does not allow or encourage the exercise of judgment with respect to how and when to hedge.

DEC does not believe that it is possible to consistently predict or profit from exchange rate movements. By locking in its entire currency exposure at the forward rate, DEC has made a judgment that the company can consistently do no better than this rate. DEC believes that using options to protect against future, unknown changes in currency risk would be unproductive because the forward rate is an accurate predictor of future currency rate moves and, on the whole, cannot be beaten.

The question of whether the currency markets are efficient and the forward rate a good indicator of what is going to happen to currency rates is beyond the scope of this book. DEC believes that they are. On the other hand, some banks and corporate currency traders have consistently racked up gains by operating as if markets could indeed be beaten. Notwithstanding, the decision about how to structure a hedging program depends largely on how management views markets and on its level of comfort with new financial strategies. At DEC, management considers markets to be efficient, and has no tolerance for financial strategies that seem to move the company in the direction of "speculating" on the movement of currencies. There is another, possibly unintentional, advantage to DEC's approach. When every transaction is hedged, and only sure transactions are hedged, then gains or losses on forward currency contracts do not show up on accounting statements. The gain or loss on hedge contracts is not reported separately; rather, it is offset against the transactions being hedged. Opportunity costs are not reported. Therefore, no one sees the effect of currency moves on the company, and no one can be blamed for what cannot be seen.

DEC's Case Against Options

DEC eschews options. On the one hand, they are considered to be speculative because they involve paying a fee in order to benefit from the opportunity of currency exchange rate shifts. On the other hand, as Downing explains, there is the cost issue:

> We have our monthly forecast data, and it shows the amount of French francs that we're expecting to receive each month over the next six months. Let's say we're expecting one hundred French francs each month. If we were very concerned that we might receive zero, then we might be nervous about taking out a forward contract. Because if we didn't receive any French francs, we'd still have to settle this contract, and in fact we would have created exposure itself. But that's not our case. We can be confident of, if not receiving one hundred francs, at least receiving ninety-five. What we want to do is not make money if the dollar weakens or speculate in that regard, but we simply want those one hundred French francs to result in a knowable number of dollars—say seventeen. You can do that with a forward. With an option what you can do is say, "That will be not less than fifteen, because I have to pay two dollars for the option," but it could be a whole lot more. When you compare the two dollars that you are paying for the option versus the possibility of how much higher it could be, you find that the present value of two is higher than the present value of possible benefits—in other words you are paying something for the option, but you pay nothing for the forward.

DEC's Case for Options

Although DEC does not consider options to be appropriate instruments for hedging transactional exposures or sales forecasts, the company does consider options to be potentially useful in hedging certain unusual types of exposure. In real estate transactions or in situations where DEC may be making a bid on future business, the company has looked at options. These are cases where prices and budgets are set today but where the actual transactions will be consummated far in the future. There may be uncertainty about when or whether the transaction will actually go through, and if a forward is used, DEC might lock itself in to a *currency hedge contract*, an obligation to deliver and receive currencies without knowing whether the underlying transaction is really going to occur. If the uncertainty is great enough, forwards can be imprudent. Under such circumstances, an option may provide hedge protection without exposing the company to additional risk.

Trading Forwards

William Davis manages the foreign exchange trading desk at Digital. He outlines the nuts and bolts of DEC's hedging system, beginning with an unambiguous statement of his mission: "We are extremely conservative in everything we do in the financial markets. We do not speculate in any way, shape, or form." The foreign exchange trading desk at DEC is not a profit center. Davis' mission is not to make money on DEC's exposures, but rather, to lock in predictability.

For example, DEC has a sales and service subsidiary in Germany, a manufacturing subsidiary in Galway, Ireland, and a rebilling company in the Netherlands. Suppose that the German sales subsidiary sells a VAX computer to a German customer. Says Davis:

> They take the order. They order the VAX from Galway. Galway sells the VAX to our rebilling center in the Netherlands, denominated in U.S. dollars. The rebilling center turns around, resells it to our German subsidiary denominated in marks. The German sub sells it in marks,

collects marks, and is not exposed on its books at all. It pays marks back to rebilling. The rebilling center has all of our European exposure.

The rebilling center buys in U.S. dollars, but the German subsidiary buys in marks, and the customer pays in marks. Thus, the paper flow shows a U.S. dollar liability and a German mark receivable. Says Davis:

> I'm hedging over here, trying to match the inflow of marks from the German sub against the hedge. It's an imperfect system. There's no hedging system that is perfect. But there is cash constantly being generated and constantly flowing back into the rebilling entity. What I do for a particular month's exposure is have a set of rolling exposures spread over the month. So I might have four or five contracts maturing during that month for German marks, and every month I'm getting a new forecast of the exposure levels from the subsidiaries.

Depending on the forecasts he receives, Davis may go to market and sell more marks forward if the exposure is growing.

DEC has a strict set of business unit hedge policies that are specific to the different operating units. Each subsidiary may have its own hardware sales business, educational services business, engineering, or various other activities depending on the region in which it does business. Davis says that while most of his hedging activity is transaction-oriented, some is anticipated sales and a smaller amount is net monetary assets.

He routinely hedges 100 percent of exposures, and will sell a currency forward at current forward rates even when he may believe it is likely to appreciate. "We're not out to make money on the currency," he emphasizes. "We're not out to speculate. Even if it looks like it may move in our favor, it may not! We are a conservative company. Our business is making and selling computers."

DEC's hedging activities give rise to a large, central portfolio, which generates gains and losses each month as it is revalued. Downing outlines the system this way:

> The French manager has a budget, a target. Let's say it's expressed in profit: we expect the French subsidiary to produce seventeen dollars of profit each month. We define that profit target in dollars, not in French francs. That's different from how many companies handle it, but that's the way we do it. In the short term if there are significant changes in the dollar-franc exchange rate, there's not a lot that the French subsidiary can do about that. Because all of the compensating actions he can take will take some time to have effect. But what we'd like to do is protect him so if he does his job he will achieve his dollar target. Say he thought the franc rate would be 6 to 1, so he knows he has to produce one hundred French francs worth of profit to produce seventeen dollars of profit. If he does that we'd like him to achieve his dollar target. If the exchange rate goes to 15 to 1, obviously he would have failed. So we'll hedge the one hundred French francs centrally and give him the gains and losses on the portfolio of French francs, so no matter what happens to the French franc rate over the six-month period, if he produces his one hundred French francs he can be guaranteed that the translation effect of the profit plus the exchange gains and losses will equal the seventeen dollars of profit.

The Buck Stops at the Dollar

DEC considers itself to be a dollar company. "Everybody in the company has the same goal," says Assistant Treasurer Paul Milbury:

> Everybody is tuned in to the dollar performance. When the dollar strengthens we want higher profits in the

subsidiaries so that we maintain the dollar returns. By measuring people in dollars rather than in French francs, we put a great deal of pressure on them to take action to bring their profits back to the dollar target.

With hedging centralized and proceeding according to a rigid discipline, DEC does not allow operating management to develop its own foreign currency hedging strategies, or to independently use such financial instruments as options, in order to enhance or protect results. As Milbury explains:

> I think back to the evolution of manufacturing in this company. When it started, we just manufactured in the United States because that's where our business was. But when we started to expand outside the United States we at Digital took a different tack from IBM. IBM decided a long time ago that for marketing reasons, it wanted to expand where its customers were and where its markets were. We at Digital, when we started to manufacture outside the United States, went for low cost. That took us to the Far East—Hong Kong, Taiwan, Singapore. It took us to Ireland, because of a combination of low cost and no taxes, and to Puerto Rico. All of that manufacturing capacity really did nothing for us in terms of balancing or neutralizing our FX exposure. On the other hand, IBM's strategy, which was not for currency but for marketing reasons, resulted in a much more balanced FX position.

DEC had actually increased its dependence on the U.S. dollar by locating manufacturing plants in countries whose own currencies were tied to the dollar. In effect, the company made a massive bet that the dollar-based competitive structure of the computer industry would continue and, what's more, that even if the competitive structure changed, the company would be better off with dollar-based manufacturing in the long run.

Digital recently has been adding some manufacturing capacity in places where the company has a large market presence. Establishing capacity in Germany, the United Kingdom, Canada, and France, besides bringing DEC closer to its customers, also has the positive effect of neutralizing the company's FX exposure through natural hedges, as discussed earlier. Tom Downing notes:

> FX exposure management was not at the top of the list of issues that drove us to put plants in those places. It was way down at the bottom of the list. But it does serve to reduce FX exposure. If we were continuing to rapidly expand our manufacturing at this point, we would probably put it where our markets are. One of the problems is that we, like most other computer manufacturers, are reducing our plant capacity because of the changes in technology in the industry. It becomes much more difficult to make the kind of strategic decisions that would result in reducing your FX exposure when you're not adding any capacity.

Operating Consequences

DEC is in a tight spot with respect to currency shifts. Operating management worldwide, constrained to return dollar budget numbers, will have to either squeeze margins or give up market share in the face of a strengthening dollar. DEC's hedging policy protects operating management from exchange rate moves that result in short-term declines in the value of local currencies against the dollar. However, DEC's hedging policy also strips out any gains that might accrue to operating management when currencies move the other way—when the dollar weakens. This creates management problems to which DEC is currently directing attention.

As Downing observes:

> I would say one of the things we want to do is make life a little bit simpler for operating managers. We want to

keep the same motivations, but the way we bring currency to the attention of management is a little bit too complex. We described how we hedge centrally and then allocate the gains and losses to subsidiaries. But when those gains and losses come to subsidiaries they're something that comes from outside. They come in a form that's pretty difficult to recognize and feel responsible for. Three years from now I would suspect that if we're successful we will have tried to increase the responsiveness of our operating units to currency by helping them develop more effective operating methods for responding to currency movements. For example, if you're buying products and raw materials in Tokyo in the yen and the yen strengthens, we'd like you to be able to move to an alternative supplier either in dollars or in some other currency. And we hope to be able to take actions like that more rapidly in the future.

Constraints on Natural Hedges and Operating Adjustments

However, one obstacle to this kind of operating response is the nature of the products that DEC is purchasing. DEC does not purchase fungible commodities. As Milbury says:

> If you were talking about gold, it doesn't matter where you buy it, gold has a certain price to it in any currency. But it's not really a pure commodity that we're dealing with; maybe if you buy from Korea it's not quite the same. Originally you decided to buy over here in the United States in dollars because it's the best product, but then the exchange rate moves and now you're ready to make a trade-off in terms of the specifications because the exchange rate has made it so attractive.

However, Downing observes that currency is just one issue among many in purchasing, and it's not the dominant one.

> Flexibility is not the sole value we're going after. You can have flexibility by having no purchasing contract at all, and solely buying spot. But you get lower prices lots of the time by locking yourself in to a long-term relationship. Also the product that a company like Digital would buy would require extensive development and customization. A lot of things that we would buy are highly tailored to Digital's requirements. So you can't change your source willy-nilly.

In order to minimize the effect of currency shifts on purchasing decisions, DEC encourages purchasing agents to buy in local currencies. Some other dollar-based companies deal with exchange rate shifts by building currency clauses into their purchasing contracts. These companies typically buy in dollars, and their purchase contracts contain clauses that allow prices to change when certain triggers are hit by the exchange rate. But DEC considers such currency clauses to be a cumbersome and ill-advised alternative to buying in local currency. As Downing explains:

> We could buy in the yen and have DEC bear the exposure or we could force the Japanese vendor into the dollar, in which case we're paying a premium price. The currency bands cause adjustment periodically to the dollar price based on the yen-dollar relationship. But it is cumbersome, because you are combining two products. One is a purchase contract and the other is a financial hedge. Sometimes you do better by separating them out.

Typically, a hedge moves inversely to the thing hedged. That is, if the currency moves one percent, the hedge gain or loss is one percent. But as Downing notes, currency clauses in purchase contracts usually operate in steps. He points out, "You can't buy contracts in the forward exchange market with steps like that, and so you've got a mismatch between your financial hedge that you can buy or sell with a bank and the hedge that's imbedded in this purchasing contract."

DEC's policy of hedging all foreign currency exposures automatically has certain disadvantages. Although the program protects operating management from a sharp spike in the dollar and allows some breathing room, the short horizon over which hedging is allowed at DEC does not provide protection against a sustained escalation in the value of the dollar.

DEC's currency risk management program emphasizes the importance of operating measures in adjusting to currency shifts. DEC considers that dollar strength and weakness can be passed on to customers in the form of price increases or reductions. Furthermore, operating managers are encouraged to diversify sourcing in order to compensate for the effects of currency exchange rate shifts on purchasing costs. Operating measures are not completely responsive to currency volatility, however. In the first place, DEC's manufacturing locations are not so located as to give maximum balance and natural hedge protection against currency moves. In the second place, the flexibility of sourcing is sometimes questionable. DEC's exacting purchase specifications mean that vendors are not easily interchangeable, especially in a two- to three-year time frame. Therefore, the company cannot quickly shift sourcing in order to take advantage of low-cost supply sources when currency exchange rates move rapidly.

With costs more or less fixed, or at least reducible only with difficulty in the short term, operating managers really have only two alternatives when currencies move: They may reduce dollar prices in order to maintain local currency prices, thus sacrificing dollar margins, or they may choose to maintain dollar price levels by raising local currency prices, with a possible result of risk to market share.

The strategy of reducing yen prices when the yen strengthens in order to maintain stable local currency export prices and retain market share has, as Professor Richard C. Marston of the Wharton

School of Business has demonstrated, worked well for the Japanese. However, Japanese exporters have an important competitive advantage that few of their non-Japanese competitors enjoy. That is, the Japanese domestic market subsidizes these strategic pricing decisions. Japanese exporters enjoy a very loyal, some would even say a "captive," domestic market. They may—and do—raise domestic yen prices when the yen strengthens. They do this in order to subsidize the yen price cuts on local currency exports.

Companies without such a buffer market may find that in the long run, approaching currency risk solely through operating measures will not work. The long run, after all, is merely a series of short runs. Managers who choose to sacrifice margins and/or market share over the short term in the expectation that long-term economic progress will prove them right may turn out to have been dead right.

Rare Competitive Structure of Industry

DEC's approach to currency risk management depends for its success on the historical competitive structure of the computer industry. The reality of this industry was that most competitors reported their results in U.S. dollars. Shareholders of computer companies are generally believed to be sensitive to the dollar value of the companies' earnings. To the extent that dollar earnings decrease because of exchange rate shifts, it is expected that shareholders will be dissatisfied. By hedging all short-term transactional exposures, DEC can protect reported earnings. As long as all major competitors set their prices on a U.S.-dollar basis, raising prices when the dollar strengthens and cutting them when the dollar falls, DEC can do the same. Therefore, it can be argued that DEC has had no competitive currency risk.

Accordingly, DEC's currency risk management program satisfies its top management's requirements that the reported quarterly P&L reflect no losses due to currency moves. In this respect, the

DEC program must be termed successful. It accomplishes the objectives for which it was designed.

However, DEC's currency risk management philosophy and system is tailored to history. Yen-based competition is increasingly a factor in the computer industry. Will DEC, like Caterpillar, wake up one day to find that a new sun has risen in its market?

CHAPTER 9

SmithKline Beckman: *Dialing for Dollars With Systems and Procedures*

SmithKline Beckman, like DEC, has little to fear from the competitive effects of currency shifts on costs and revenues. This is a consequence of the competitive structure of the pharmaceutical industry. However, the absence of currency-related competitive threats to the business does not mean an absence of currency risk. While DEC's risk management system aims to remove the exercise of human judgment from the risk management process, SmithKline Beckman has installed batteries of automated systems in order to encourage and exploit the best judgment of its risk managers. An active user of a variety of instruments, SmithKline Beckman aims to maximize the value of its currency

portfolio and minimize costs of hedging. Smith-
Kline's value maximizing approach to risk management resembles the approach taken at Union Carbide (see Chapter 6). However, SmithKline
Beckman does not treat currency management as a
revenue-generating activity or as a profit center.
Thus, this story exemplifies a middle ground between the active cultivation of risk in a profit center
approach and the utter elimination of apparent risk
in a hedge-it-all approach, while examining closely
the extent to which automated systems can facilitate the risk manager's exercise of judgment.

No Role for Operating Adjustments

Multinational pharmaceutical companies are different from the
kinds of companies previously discussed. Operating responses to
currency shifts hardly enter their strategies at all. This is not a
matter of choice. The industry is research driven. New products are
what send stock prices soaring.

In most countries, when the products come to market, pricing
is a matter of negotiation between the company and the government. Direct cost is not quite a negligible factor, but neither is it
terribly important. Few sick people will prefer to use a cheaper,
less-effective drug because they can save 20 percent off the price of
a costly miracle cure. Furthermore, patents protect pharmaceutical
companies' unique products from direct competition. We hear of
comparably equipped automobiles; we do not hear of comparably
equipped drugs. Competitive risk is not an issue. However, prices
cannot be increased to pass along effects of currency moves either.

So there is little that a pharmaceutical can do operationally to
cope with the effects of currency rate swings. Because the industry
is not subject to ordinary kinds of competitive and economic
constraints, management of foreign exchange risk is largely a matter
of maximizing the dollar value of local currency earnings. Currency

risk management for pharmaceutical companies means managing financial flows with financial instruments and financial strategies. It is system-intensive. SmithKline Beckman is a case in point.

History

Through mergers with Allergan in 1980 and with Beckman in 1982, Philadelphia-based SmithKline developed into a Fortune 100 multinational corporation with sales in well over one hundred countries. In 1989, SmithKline Beckman agreed to merge with Beecham of the United Kingdom. As this book goes to press, details of the merger are being worked out. During the decade of the 1980s, however, the currency risk management function at SKB grew—in size, importance, and sophistication—as the mergers brought additional ongoing export sales and overseas manufacturing and selling operations, as well as international growth of the original core business.

Diversity Complicates Management

The SmithKline Beckman program of exposure management aims to take maximum advantage of currency moves while keeping currency threats at a level acceptable to the overall business. Beginning with the definition of the company's exposures, a definition clarified and enhanced by a comprehensive, computerized exposure measurement and monitoring system, SmithKline Beckman proceeds along a two-pronged path to both minimize and strategically manage currency risk.

The diversity of SmithKline Beckman's businesses complicates this task. SKB's instrument business, for example, relies heavily on U.S.-based manufacturing. Most of the instrument division's overseas subsidiaries are sales subsidiaries, purchasing product from the U.S. manufacturing centers for distribution worldwide. A realignment in currencies could be life or death to that business because manufacturing costs are a major component of pricing and competition in the instrument industry.

On the other hand, the pharmaceutical business is far less subject to the competitive effects of currency moves. In the first place, much of SmithKline Beckman's production for the European market is centered in Ireland, and the Irish currency generally moves together with the other European currencies. In the second place, manufacturing costs are not a heavy factor in determining the sales prices in the pharmaceutical business.

Furthermore, pharmaceutical prices are controlled in most countries. Says Stephen Hendrix, Vice-President and Assistant Treasurer of SmithKline Beckman, who is responsible for currency risk management, "Drugs are patented. Uniqueness is a more important characteristic than the production cost. But the translation of earnings into U.S. dollars is critical." Therefore, SmithKline Beckman's exposure in the pharmaceutical division is for the most part accounting exposure of U.S.-dollar–reported earnings.

Technology-Intensive Approach

Yet SmithKline Beckman's approach to managing its exposures is not as simple as merely hedging everything automatically in order to lock in book values. Rather, this company recognizes that there is ample room for the application of sound judgment to the problem of optimizing performance on the floating battlefield. SmithKline Beckman's battery of computerized systems includes historical analysis of the effect of exchange rate moves on the company's business in the past and several scenarios for the probable effect of future moves on any given exposure.

Identifying Exposures

SmithKline Beckman recently overhauled and fine-tuned its foreign exchange management system. As the dollar weakened in the post-

1985 period, the company questioned how much of its improved performance was attributable to the currency effect. Management knew that it was benefiting from the weak dollar, but it had not quantified the impact. Says Hendrix, "We knew the dollar was not going to continue down forever. The question in everybody's mind was, What was the true impact to earnings? It was benefiting us, but we didn't know exactly by how much."

Translation Exposures

For SmithKline Beckman, translation exposure is very close to what some companies consider to be economic exposure. Others call it cash flow exposure. Terminology in the field of corporate currency risk management is not yet standardized. But the concepts behind the terminology are recognizable. So, SKB's foreign exchange director, James Johnson, observes:

> We have found that the hardest thing for management to understand is the distinction between transaction and translation. Most people understand transaction exposure; it's on the books, it's reported, and everyone can see it. But translation exposure can appear anywhere in the accounting statements. For example, say we were shipping to England and the first month our receivables are getting $1.60 per pound sterling; but two months later our receivables are only getting $1.55. We are receiving less dollars for the goods we are shipping out, and the cost of those goods has not changed but our dollar return has changed. It doesn't show up anywhere except on the very bottom line of the company, where you say, "Our company's income has diminished."

Translation exposures, as the term is used at SmithKline Beckman, include both economic/competitive exposure as well as straightforward reporting exposures. British assets translated at the rate of $1.60 per pound sterling in year one and $1.55 in year two have lost value. But this loss in value is not related to the economics of the business in the United Kingdom. If costs and revenues are based in pounds, the effect of converting them into dollars for reporting purposes is merely a bookkeeping exercise. However, when costs are in dollars and revenues in pounds, a change in the relative value of dollars and pounds has real economic effect because it will increase or decrease costs and revenues.

Currency risk affects the instrument division in a different way. If the U.S.-dollar-based instrument division sells to Italy, the Italian cost of goods sold is based on U.S. dollars. Therefore, if the lira devalues, it buys fewer dollars. In order to pay the bills from the U.S. instrument division, the Italian sales subsidiary must earn more lira—or sacrifice margin. A price increase may be necessary; otherwise, such local costs as advertising and labor must be cut. The effect on the company is a real economic effect. It affects the ability of the business to maintain competitive strength. Says Johnson, "Whenever there's a change in alignment there's a change in profit. So we're looking at this as an exposure that needs to be managed, because it has a direct impact on profits."

Transactional Exposures

The next major area of exposure management at SmithKline Beckman addresses is *transactional exposures*. Here, the company differentiates between transactions within the group of companies comprising this multinational corporation (intercompany transactions) and transactions with companies outside the group (third-party transactions). The distinction is important because many of the intercompany transactions are subjected to a netting program, which is described at length later in this chapter.

Hyperinflationary Exposures

Hyperinflationary exposures are defined by accounting regulations, specifically FASB 52. This regulation requires that the business transacted by subsidiaries based in hyperinflationary countries be accounted for on a U.S. dollar basis. In other words, any change in the value of local currency net monetary assets and liabilities flows through the income statement. As Johnson notes, "All changes in your balance sheet go through your P&L and when you're dealing in a hyperinflationary climate your assets are changing very rapidly. That's a big factor."

Equity Exposures

The final area of currency exposure identified at SmithKline Beckman is *equity exposure*. This is what most companies mean when they talk about translation gains or losses. Under current accounting regulations, changes in the value of foreign equity because of exchange rate moves affect a special account in the shareholders' equity section of the balance sheet. Except in hyperinflationary countries, as noted earlier, these changes do not pass through the income statement.

Data Collection and Reports

After exposures were defined, the SKB team moved to develop a comprehensive measurement system. This system collects data and spews out reports that quantify exposures in each major category enumerated above. Transaction exposures are identified and measured by regular reports from overseas subsidiaries. Major subsidiaries use standardized forms to send required information about the level of receivables and payables on their balance sheets by currency. These reports go through General Electric (GE)'s worldwide computer network, and are downloaded to a personal computer-driven data base program at SmithKline Beckman's Philadelphia headquarters.

The program develops a cross-currency matrix, which tells SKB's currency team not only the exposures of each subsidiary to the local currency and the dollar but also the cross-currency exposures. For example, if a German subsidiary is selling to an Italian company, there is an exposure: a cross-currency exposure between the German mark and the Italian lira. The economic effects discussed earlier in the context of the U.S. dollar and the British pound are no less valid with respect to the German mark and the Italian lira, or the French franc and the Dutch guilder.

Of course, both the German mark and the Italian lira are constituent currencies of the EMS, and generally move together with respect to the U.S. dollar. However, from time to time there are realignments of currencies within the EMS. The lira may weaken or strengthen; its value as expressed in German marks or French francs or Dutch guilders can change. By monitoring cross-currency exposures, SKB can take prudent management action to hedge EMS currencies against each other when that is advisable. The matrix categorizes EMS cross-currency exposures as "strong to strong" and "strong to weak." "We pick out our exposure and we cover it," says Hendrix.

A second computer program also identifies and forecasts translation exposure. It uses GE's worldwide network, but the data are downloaded into SKB's mainframe. Hendrix explains:

> Each of our foreign companies fills in a balance sheet. It's the same format that we use for financial reporting so that our companies overseas can immediately identify with it. [They] are used to providing numbers. We ask for last year's actual and for the current-month actual. They report what they have on the books and they report a forecast at a minimum of three months going out; then we write forecasts going out by month for several months, then for the year, then for a couple more periods at the end of the following year. We do this for each country, and then the computer takes all the data and comes up with summary reports.

Forecasting Model

No line item on a financial statement identifies the effect of exchange rates on a company's economic strength or value. The effect of exchange rate shifts on cost of goods sold or on sales revenues is not broken out and reported separately. Therefore, in order to properly quantify these effects, SKB has developed a model.

Cost-of-goods-sold and earnings figures for each of SmithKline Beckman's 132 subsidiary companies are the input data. The cost-of-goods-sold figure does not include dollar costs, say for inventory sourced from the United States, because dollar currency costs do not comprise a foreign currency exposure. That portion of cost of goods sold that will rise and fall when exchange rates shift is an exposure, and is input. Furthermore, the system is refined enough to include an inventory lag in order to allow for goods purchased and put into inventory before the rates shift. The model permits an analyst to alter the inventory lag so as to factor in the inventory management decisions that local operating units may have taken to respond to economic factors, including the exchange rate environment.

Says Hendrix:

> We then take an entire matrix for transaction exposure of all the payments of 132 companies making payments to another 132 companies. So you've got a 132-by-132 matrix of the intercompany payables and receivables. We then add third-party payments, and we calculate the hyperinflationary exposure and our equity position. Then we input all our book exchange rates both for income statement and for balance sheet purposes. Book rates are the monthly rates that are set at the end of each month and are used for conversion of our balance sheets and P&Ls by the accountants. As the exchange rates change, the computer takes the change times of each one of the exposures by its respective currencies and then accumulates all that info by country, by currency, in the business

units, in the currency blocs, and finally in the one net number which says what the impact has been on the company in one period—say this year versus last year—so we know what the cost has been. That's half the model. In order to properly measure the effect of exchange rate shifts on earnings and on competitiveness, the program has a two-year historical "memory."

The second half of the model is prospective, it's a forecast. We input the forecast numbers for each of those categories—the translation exposures, the transaction exposures, the hyperinflationary and the equity numbers—and then we put this into the computer. What happens if the mark moves 5 percent or 10 percent? What is the impact on the company? It takes that percentage change and calculates on each one of the exposures what the impact will be by currency and country, on a business unit, on a currency block, and then on the whole company. It does it in ten seconds.

So, at the end of the day, SKB management knows what the historical effects have been of a given change in the exchange rate. They also have a picture of what is likely to happen in the future under several scenarios. The model allows treasury decision makers at SmithKline Beckman to manage exposures and develop strategies in the light of comprehensive, detailed, and continuously updated information about the effect of their decisions and the decisions of operating management in an unpredictable currency environment.

Consolidation

The first step in managing foreign currency exposures is to consolidate them. SmithKline Beckman consolidates its short-term transaction exposures through a computerized trading and *netting* system. A number of U.S. companies have established in Europe and in Asia reinvoicing centers that effectively minimize transaction exposures by netting them out. Generally, an office in London, Belgium, or Singapore is established to handle the paper flow on intercompany sales. All intercompany sales are made to this reinvoicing center, as are all intercompany purchases. With sales invoices and purchasing remittances flowing into one concentration point, companies consolidate their intercompany transaction exposures, making them more manageable.

However, SmithKline Beckman has advanced the art of trading and netting by establishing a worldwide system based in a PC located on a desk top in Philadelphia. Each subsidiary reports monthly by electronic mail what intercompany payments it will be making that month and to what entity. Typically, the number of payments may approach 400. Without the netting system, each subsidiary would have to make separate bank arrangements for each of the 400 payments. With the system, a treasury staffer in Philadelphia consolidates all payments in each currency and informs subsidiaries whether they are in a net pay or a net receive position.

Meanwhile, for each of the nineteen currency accounts, the system nets payments and receipts. Each subsidiary is directed to pay its own net payment obligation to the netting center, which in turn pays the net receipts due to other subsidiaries. Each subsidiary pays and receives in payment its own local currency, except in a few countries where there are government foreign exchange controls. Thus, the system has taken a total of 400 intercompany payments down to forty or fifty payments. Furthermore, with the net transaction exposure centralized in Philadelphia, treasury can manage it in the light of currency market developments, buying or selling currencies as required, to balance the net amount of transaction exposure. Generally, the goal of the netting center is to "zero out" each of the nineteen currency accounts.

Johnson explains the advantages in these terms:

> What it does for the entities is, instead of making five or six payments in five or six currencies, they make one payment in their own local currency; and instead of receiving five or six payments in five or six currencies,

they receive one payment in their local currency. So it takes away the need for the local entity going out and entering into a lot of foreign exchange transactions, some of which would be very small, and making payments into a lot of different bank accounts. What it does for us on a bigger scale is that we're able to take all the currencies, throw them into the pot, and decide what the net amount is we need to buy ourselves to balance the pot.

The netting procedure is made more efficient by international cash pools. Many companies have, in the United States or overseas, a cash concentration account. Companies that are part of the same consolidated tax group pool their borrowing requirements and their excess cash in a single bank account. If the account has a surplus cash position, it is automatically invested overnight. If there is a deficit, the account automatically borrows from either the bank or some other source. Then, in the morning, the various companies in the group receive their net cash positions.

However, Hendrix notes that this system causes commingling of corporate accounts for tax purposes.

We want to keep those accounts separate on the banks' books, so in every country except Japan, we tell the banks we want to set up an arrangement where they combine the debits and credits on a memo basis. Money doesn't flow into one common account. The accounts are separate but the computer adds them up as if they were one account and gives us credit if there's surplus or charges us if there's an overdraft. So our cash pools (except for Japan, where you can't do that) are all on a memo basis.

This system has several advantages for short-term currency management. For example, in Germany, SmithKline may have excess cash in one subsidiary, but a deficit in another. Without a cash pool, the deficit would be covered by bank borrowing. In effect, SmithKline would be borrowing its own cash. Pooling eliminates bank spreads. Investment and borrowing are automatic. The cash pool also speeds up netting. Even in countries where subsidiaries might otherwise have a problem meeting their netting payments because of FX regulations or availability, they can draw on the pool to reimburse the netting center. Johnson notes:

> They don't have to say, "How about we delay it until next Tuesday when I have the money?" There's immediate cash availability. We've found that you really cannot isolate foreign exchange management from the rest of your operations. Good international cash management is integral to your management of exposures. If you can move the cash from where it is to where you want it economically, it will facilitate keeping your exposures low.

Examples

Currency risk management at SmithKline Beckman is best illustrated through an example.

The company has routinely protected the *netting value*—that is, the value of foreign currencies in the nineteen currency netting accounts—through option strategies. A buyer of an option pays a fee, known as a premium, in return for the right, but not the obligation, to buy or sell a particular currency for a set price during a set period of time. Options that give the right to buy are named *call options*. Options that confer the right to sell are named *put options*.

Proxy Hedging With Options

Because the European currencies usually move together in the EMS, SKB is willing to use the German mark as a proxy currency to hedge the EMS currencies. Options on the Italian lira and the

Spanish peseta are expensive. An option to buy or sell the German mark is considerably less expensive, and because the German mark and the other EMS currencies move together against the U.S. dollar, the German mark can be used to hedge other EMS currencies.

Using the German mark as a proxy for the EMS netting exposure of SmithKline Beckman, Johnson, over one four-month period, bought put options and sold call options. At the time, the dollar was rising and the European currencies were falling. To ensure that the European currencies would translate to a healthy sum of dollars, he bought put options; these gave him the right to sell marks for an attractive dollar price. However, because the put option was expensive and he wanted to reduce the price, Johnson entered into another transaction: He sold a call option.

The call option gave the buyer the right to purchase German marks from SmithKline Beckman at a certain price. The premium that Johnson collected when he sold the call option helped offset the premium he had paid to purchase the put option. The put option gave him assurance that he could protect himself against a continued weakening of the European currency position, but it allowed him to benefit if the European currencies strengthened. At some point, if they strengthened enough, the party who had bought his call option would exercise the option and buy the German marks. However, Johnson did not believe that the European currencies would strengthen that far, and the premium he received gave him an immediate benefit.

This option strategy allowed SmithKline Beckman to eliminate the risk of a strengthening dollar while retaining opportunity to profit if the dollar happened to weaken. The income from selling the call option reduced the net cost of this hedge to about 40 percent of what a normal put premium would be. Says Johnson:

> The way it turned out was that the cap was fine. The dollar started to come off, but it never went below the call. So we put a cap on, we minimized the cost of that

cap, and when the dollar came off we were able to capture the gain.

Hedging an Acquisition With Options and Forwards

Another example occurred in connection with a major acquisition in Japan. SmithKline Beckman owned 50 percent of a joint venture company, and management decided to negotiate for purchasing the remaining 50 percent. "At this point the dollar was under tremendous pressure," Johnson relates, "but the negotiations were still in a very early stage. So we decided to take out call options. That put a floor on the dollar value of the cost of what we anticipated it would be to purchase the shares." By summer, it was certain that the negotiations were going to be successful: By this time the yen had weakened; the options had lost a lot of their value; it was economical to take out forwards. The forward price of yen was lower than the strike price on the options that SmithKline Beckman had bought.

Hendrix explains:

> It was still a conservative strategy. We didn't want the purchase cost to be more expensive in dollars than the strike price on the option. Here we were sitting with this contingent liability, we liked the price that we got on the strike price, then the liability became firm, so we had an opportunity to buy the yen outright. The options are worth considerably less because the yen has weakened considerably. The company is better off economically, but here we still had the options. So we kept the options, which again is conservative. What's the point of selling them? They're not worth much, and if the yen does move back, then you've got a gain. It can't hurt the company.

In other words, if it made sense to make this acquisition at the strike price plus the cost of the option premium, once the yen weakened and they knew that they were going to make the purchase, the company could save money by purchasing the yen forward.

Despite the weakening of the yen, which had caused the options to lose most of their value, there was a possibility that the yen could appreciate. Rather than closing out the option position by selling the options for what the market would pay—not much—SmithKline Beckman decided to keep them. An appreciation in the yen would make them more valuable.

In fact, the appreciation did occur. According to Johnson, "The yen strengthened to the strike price of the options. At that point we were really double covered. So instead of maintaining double cover, we then took the profits on the forward contracts."

So, the company had made a profit on the forward position, and still had the option contract in place. "The yen then weakened again," says Johnson, "weakened dramatically, and we were in the same situation we had been in before. It made sense to enter into a forward contract."

So the company again bought forward contracts at the cheap prevailing rate.

> Then the yen dramatically strengthened again beyond the strike price, and by this time the time value was getting pretty short, we were now entering into the last month of the contracts, we took the profits on the option contracts. The option contracts gave us the basis to do the things we did, all based on economics, because of the flexibility of option contracts.

"And," Hendrix stresses:

> It's all conservative. You're not exposing the company to risk, as you can see if you go through the scenario in each case. You have to separate how these options are used, which is in the form of insurance, and you pay a premium and you get protection if the exchange rates move.

The strategy paid off in a big way. SmithKline Beckman saved about 20 percent on the total cost of the Japanese acquisition.

Calculating Impact of Risk

Using the computerized exposure measurement system reviewed earlier, treasury staff at SKB can report to management the consequences of exchange rate moves on various corporate objectives. If the risk is the risk of a rising dollar, the measurement system can report and quantify its potential impact on an annual basis to the company. "Then we have to look at the costs from there," says Johnson. "What does it cost to give us the proper protection? It's impact, potential risk, and cost."

Impact and potential risk may be calculated in two ways. One is a probability weighted forecast. For example, if the current exchange rate for German marks is 1.83 marks to each dollar, Hendrix explains, "Say we think there's a 25 percent probability it could be 1.87, or maybe a 30 percent probability it will be 1.78. We'll look and draw our curve going out, and taking each of the probabilities by each of the numerical gains and losses will give us a net overall position."

"The other way to do it is to use our budget rates," says Johnson.

> When we forecast for the coming year where we think exchange rates will be at given times during the year, and that is agreed upon internally, we say to management, "This is your target, this is what you have tasked the operations to produce, so much in earnings, we can deliver that to you, but the cost is going to be such and so depending on which hedging instrument you use."

SmithKline Beckman considers a full range of financial instruments in its risk management program. "Everything is explored," says Hendrix. "We look at forwards and options, at swaps, at foreign borrowings, etc."

For purposes of managing short-term risk, risk that is contained within the yearly budget cycle, forwards and options are most often the instrument of choice. When forwards, and when options? Johnson explains:

> That would be based upon cost and what we're trying to accomplish. Options are generally expensive. We look at a lot of option scenarios. We've also looked at how to get the cost of an option within the range that we feel comfortable with. For example, we will buy a put and then sell a call deep into the money. We've also looked at using the German mark for a proxy for our expensive-to-hedge currencies like the lira and the peseta. This gets the cost down dramatically.

Accounting for such creative hedging positions is difficult, for reasons discussed in Chapter 3. Accounting regulations penalize economically sound risk management decisions. Hendrix notes, "Our auditors today are taking a conservative point of view. We can account for options that we purchase as a financial investment. So it would be the lower of cost or market. For anything that we write we would have to report all losses that exceed the premium received."

Debt Swaps

Longer-term, multiyear exposures such as equity investments may be managed through swaps and long-term foreign currency borrowings. A *swap* is an agreement to exchange cash payments of principal and interest on loans denominated in different currencies. Says Johnson:

> We would designate a swap as a hedge against equity position. But we would only do a swap on a currency

where we get a net interest differential that is positive to the U.S. dollar—for example the German mark or the Japanese yen. We can borrow yen at approximately half the cost of a dollar borrowing.

Borrowing against equity effectively locks in the U.S. dollar value of investments in place. Any foreign exchange gain or loss on the loan is offset by gain or loss on the equity position. Some companies also use such borrowings to take advantage of favorable foreign interest rates. They may borrow yen, which they do not need but which are available at a low interest rate, and convert the proceeds into dollars, or they may enter a swap in order to obtain dollars but pay the lower interest rate for borrowing yen. Current accounting regulations usually require foreign currency borrowings to be reported as speculative, and any gain or loss is forced to flow through the P&L. However, a company with a net foreign equity position in Japan can borrow yen at favorable low interest rates, designate the borrowing as a hedge of the equity position, and avoid any P&L affect. "It's a wash," says Hendrix. "It goes through your equity; that's part of your cumulative translation adjustment." The advantage to the corporation is that the cost of funds is much lower because the company is paying lower interest rates.

U.S. companies with Japanese competitors may use a similar approach to protect themselves somewhat against a strengthening dollar. By borrowing yen when the yen is strong, and converting the proceeds into dollars when the dollar is weak, U.S. companies can share a cost advantage available to their Japanese competitors. When the dollar strengthens against the yen, the U.S. companies can use their strong dollar revenues to pay off their weak yen financing. To the extent that financing costs are an important cost to the corporation, this measure helps them to compete, by cutting the cost of financing. On the other hand, when the yen strengthens against the dollar, the cost of financing goes up. However, since the Japanese competitors' financing costs will also go up, and since the U.S. company may have many other costs not tied to the yen (labor, materials, energy) and which enjoy a favorable competitive effect when the yen strengthens, this type of strategic borrowing may operate as an effective competitive hedge.

Hendrix observes:

> The markets are changing, the exposures are changing, the hedging instruments are constantly being invented and improved. We have developed a system that allows us to look at a particular hedging strategy, calculate the gain or loss, then bring it all together. So if we look at one particular strategy, we know what the gain or loss is going to be, the total effect, depending on the movement of the currency.

Given the amount of analytical and systems support available to the company, one might expect that SmithKline Beckman would trade currencies for profit to beat the markets, judging the performance of its hedging program by how well and how consistently it turns in positive returns. Nothing could be further from the truth. Says Hendrix:

> We want our position to be profitable, but if we spend a lot of time developing short-term trading profits, then our attention will focus on the very short-term profit swings and it will not be as focused on the income streams and the trend in the operations and the long-term movements of the markets. On the other hand, we would be very reluctant to try to take out long-term hedges beyond a year because we're not certain to make a profit on something like that.

Although the subsidiary companies report once a month, Hendrix and his staff of two do not necessarily hedge the positions at the same time or in the same way.

> Since the numbers always tend to average around a certain level, we always have a feel for what our exposures

are. So it's a matter of looking and seeing where the markets are and knowing where we don't want to be in terms of FX rates and then devising the instrument that's appropriate.

The timing is determined by the market rather than by the position. The position is, in a sense, an ongoing business. SKB has two perspectives on the position: a 12-month annual plan for actions in given scenarios, and the very short term, monthly netting exposures.

Conclusion

In the preceding pages, we have looked closely at several approaches to the management of currency risk. Here, let us review the basic principles of currency risk management that may be induced from the examples and case studies that have gone before.

Money and Currency

Money is purchasing power. Resources purchased with money are an essential input into almost every manufacturing or service function. Money can only be thought about, spoken about, or used when it takes the form of currency. When economists in the United States address the "money supply," they are really addressing the dollar supply. The dollar supply has an impact on the price of dollars relative to other currencies, other measures of purchasing power, and other names of money—yen, marks, pound sterling. This is true because, within the industrial world, all currencies may be substituted and exchanged one for the other. The exchange is not always legal. However, even in countries where it is illegal to exchange currencies, there is still a price at which the exchange can and usually does take place.

Therefore, the costs of manufacturing in the United States may be expressed in yen or in marks just as the costs of running a hotel in Tokyo may be expressed in pound sterling or in dollars. Any German or Japanese automobile manufacturer contemplating an investment in the United States evaluates the investment ultimately in the home currency just as any British or North American hotelier does when considering a joint venture in Japan. This is why currency risk affects every company. Every company may be said to do business in marks, yen, dollars, and pound sterling simultaneously. The resources each business consumes and produces may be measured in money, and money may be thought of in terms of many different currencies. Every business receives and pays money, but calls it by different names. Money is a measure of purchasing power. Purchasing power may be measured as dollars, yen, pound sterling, or any other currency.

Managing Resources Means Managing Currencies

Many business managers act as if money had only one name, the name they call it when they buy and sell resources. In the United States, for example, money is called *dollar*. However, *dollar* is not money's full name. Acting as though the dollar meant money and money meant the dollar leads to bad management decisions. The global market harshly punishes bad management decisions of this sort.

At the heart of currency risk is the problem of calling money by its proper name. This differs from industry to industry and from company to company. Money's name is seldom the name of a single national currency. Although money's common names differ from country to country, this difference is usually almost as insignificant for business as the colors that tint countries on a map of the world. Money's proper name is the name of a relationship, the relationship between currencies that matter to the business.

Take the example of a U.S. manufacturer who pays for all of its materials in dollars, pays its work force in dollars, and sells its product to other American customers who also pay for it in dollars. This manufacturer has grown used to thinking of money as dollars. Suppose that this manufacturer emphasizes cost cutting as an ongoing business policy. If this manufacturer manages to reduce overall costs by 15 percent over a three-year period, it may think it has become more competitive. After all, it costs fewer dollars, and therefore less money, to get its product out the door. However, if the dollar has strengthened by 35 percent over the same period, what has the manufacturer really accomplished?

Competitive Risk

The manufacturer may have accomplished a great deal or it may have gone backward. The competitive structure of the industry will determine the answer. We have reviewed the steps that Chrysler has taken to answer this question for itself. Chrysler is a North American company. After the divestitures of the 1970s, Chrysler had, for practical purposes, no international costs or sales. Yet Chrysler discovered that in its business, managing money really meant managing resources measured in terms of both dollars and yen. If the dollar becomes stronger than the yen, then Chrysler will face a competitive problem.

Management for Chrysler includes managing the relationship of the dollar and the yen in order to protect the company from incurring a competitive disadvantage from changes in the relationship between the dollar and the yen. The impact of currency risk hits Chrysler as a relative cost differential. Purchasing departments have always been tasked with controlling dollar purchasing costs;

production departments have always searched for dollar cost-effective processes and plant sites; marketing departments have always attempted to optimize dollar pricing, to price with an eye to costs and also to demand. Chrysler has learned, though, that purchasing cannot think in dollars alone and has designed into its purchasing program a process for controlling the competitive effect of currency on the company. Among the components of this program are diversification of sourcing and hedging with financial instruments.

Caterpillar is another company whose management sees currency as a competitive factor. Caterpillar has had to address the effect of currency values on purchasing costs. However, the marketing impact of currency risk has also been important for Caterpillar. It has had to think about currencies not only with regard to their impact on production costs and U.S.-dollar-denominated sales but also with regard to their impact on sales by distributors in many countries and economies. Because Caterpillar's dealers receive revenues in various currencies, Caterpillar and its dealers also have to pay attention to how currencies affect prices in various currencies. But this effect is not simple. Caterpillar's pricing is, after all, part of the competitive strategy to outmaneuver Komatsu. Therefore, its pricing must take into account not only the relationship between the dollar and the local customer's currency but the relationship—still paramount despite Caterpillar's diversification of currency cost—of the dollar and the yen as this relationship is reflected in the local currency.

For both Caterpillar and Chrysler, two companies that used to think exclusively in terms of the dollar, managing resources now means managing the relationship between the dollar and the yen because that relationship matters to their businesses. The management of money, of the dollar-yen relationship, is a task with operational and competitive impact. The management of currency risk, therefore, is not merely a treasury function. The management of currency risk enters into the jobs of purchasing managers, marketing managers, production managers, dealers, and others.

Corporate managers, of course, cannot manage the relationship between the dollar and the yen in any overwhelming, macro-

economic sense. However, they can manage the relationship between the dollar and the yen at the point where that relationship
intersects with their business. Put differently, they can manage their
business in such a way as to make the impact of the dollar-yen
relationship work for them.

This can be done through both financial and operating actions, a point to which we shall return.

Economic Risk

The effect of currency moves on a company is not always competitive. However, almost every company facing foreign competitors,
competitors who manufacture their product or measure their results
in a different currency, has competitive currency risks—far more
than have thought of it.

Notwithstanding, just as there are 100 percent domestic companies with enormous exposures to competitive currency risk, so
also are there cosmopolitan, multinational companies with no
competitive currency risk—that is, the relationship between currencies does not determine the competitive strength or weakness of
these companies. However, these companies have other kinds of
currency risk—for example that the foreign currency earnings of
their businesses will become more or less valuable in home currency terms because of currency moves. SmithKline Beckman and
Digital Equipment Corporation are among the companies that have
this kind of risk.

When the risk is of a short-term nature—that is, when revenues on a particular sale are likely to be more or less valuable
because of currency moves that occur between the time the sale is
booked and the time the receivable is collected—it's called a
transactional risk. It is a risk affecting a particular transaction.

When the risk is longer-term—for example, the risk that a
one- or two- or three-year sales and earnings forecast may be
derailed because of currency moves—then it is called economic
risk. Economic risk is not quite the same thing as competitive risk;

competitive risk is the risk that a company will fare less well in competition because of currency shifts. However, a company may have economic risk even if it has no competitors but has foreign currency earnings.

Among the companies whose currency risk management programs figure in the preceding chapters are Digital Equipment Corporation and SmithKline Beckman. Neither company has had to cope with competitive currency risks—*to date*. Digital Equipment Corporation operates a business in an industry that was born and grew up in the United States. Computers have historically been dominated by U.S. manufacturers. Pricing has historically been in dollars, so when the dollar has strengthened or weakened with respect to other currencies, the effect could simply be passed on to the buyer. In addition, computers are not bought on the basis of price so much as on their technical and performance characteristics. Price may be important, but it is not the determining factor in a decision to buy this brand or the other. Therefore, when the prices of U.S. computer companies' products rose because of a shift in the value of the dollar, the buyers did not rush to substitute cheaper Japanese or French or German or British products. Because U.S. companies historically dominated the technical competition in the computer industry, it followed that the dollar dominated the pricing competition. Therefore, DEC has not had competitive currency risk. Although there is considerable question as to whether this competitive structure will continue to prevail in the computer industry, there is no question that it has been a historical reality.

SmithKline Beckman, a large pharmaceutical company, has no appreciable competitive currency risk either. Pharmaceutical companies compete not on the basis of price but on the basis of unique products with unique performance characteristics. Products are patented; furthermore, prices are controlled in most markets. An increase in material or production costs generally has a minor, not to say negligible, effect on the ability of a pharmaceutical company to move its product into the market. Sick people do not generally shop for price but for a cure. Therefore, SmithKline Beckman does not have competitive currency risk.

In the cases of DEC and SmithKline Beckman, it is the competitive structure of the industry that determines their freedom from competitive currency risk. All of DEC's main competitors have historically been American, and pricing has historically been dominated by the dollar. And competitive currency risk does not exist for SmithKline Beckman. The reason for this is that pharmaceutical companies operate in an unusual industry that is protected by patents and pricing in a context of government regulation.

However, because they are selling internationally, and collecting revenues in foreign currencies, both DEC and SmithKline Beckman have transactional and economic risks. Both companies take care to address their transactional risks through financial hedging programs as elaborate as they are different. With respect to longer-term economic risks, SmithKline Beckman relies primarily on financial hedges, while DEC relies primarily on operating measures and endeavors to establish natural hedges.

Identifying Risk

In order to identify currency risk, managers must first look at the competitive structure of their industry. They should begin by bringing together representatives of both financial and operating areas in order to review what has happened to purchasing costs, production costs, and sales revenue under different exchange rate scenarios.

The purpose of this exercise is to determine how currency risk has affected the company in the past. For example, if an American company suffered greatly during the early 1980s but has found life to be much easier since 1985, that is a good indication that the business depends heavily on currency relationships. In other words, the company has a heavy exposure to one or more currencies other than its home currency.

Analyzing the company's cost and revenue history in the light of exchange rate moves will give management part of the story, but not all of it. There can be several reasons why results have changed when currency values have changed.

It is imperative that the company know what the real reasons are. If it has a competitive risk, then a strategy must be developed to address that risk, one that necessarily takes into account what the competitors are expected to do.

Therefore, the currency risk task force should examine who the company's competitors are. Financial analysts should go through annual reports and other information about the competition in order to determine how historical changes in currency rates have affected competitors. If competitors have not been affected, they need to ask, Why not?

The answer may be illuminating, but it's unlikely to be contained in the annual report. It will probably be related to where the competition sources, manufactures, and sells—information that is usually available from industry sources. Purchasing staff may obtain some of it from vendors. Sales staff usually know the other players in their market and how well each is doing. Newspapers, magazines, trade journals, and other publications often contain short announcements about new plants or about marketing initiatives. Published sources can be searched quickly and inexpensively by an on-line service.

Once the company has assembled data about itself and the competition, it is possible to answer some questions about how currency shifts affect the competitive situation. For example, the American company may have done very poorly in the early 1980s but extremely well since 1985. Assuming that the competitor is Japanese, analysis may show that the competitor did very well in the early 1980s and perhaps a little less well after 1985. If the Japanese competitor is known to have begun buying more from Korea and Taiwan (whose currencies are linked to the dollar) and also to have put up a new manufacturing facility in North America, it is fair to say that the competitor has benefited from having established natural hedges.

This means that the competitor is well-positioned to weather shifts in the dollar-yen relationship. It can probably shift sourcing from Taiwan and Korea back to Japan if the yen weakens. On the other hand, when the yen strengthens, the competitor can use the manufacturing capacity located in the United States to serve the American market.

If this kind of profile emerges, the American company must seriously examine how well it has positioned itself. Many managers will find that they are positioned very inadequately. For example, a number of companies established offshore sourcing arrangements when the dollar was strong, and a number established overseas manufacturing facilities, but most companies did not carefully consider how their sourcing arrangements affected their currency exposures. If we continue with our example of an American company facing a Japanese competitor, it is safe to say that the American company's currency exposure is not helped at all by additional sourcing from countries whose currencies are pegged to the dollar.

It may be that the American company is in an industry where competitors are all American, so that the change in currency values over the past decade has not affected sales or costs at all. It may also be that the industry in which the company operates is like pharmaceuticals, where patents protect companies from head-to-head competition and costs have little to do with pricing. If the company does not have competitive currency risk, then the currency risk task force should address the issue of whether there are other kinds of threats or opportunities that may emerge from currency exchange rate shifts.

It may be that the company has made or is planning to make acquisitions in other countries. If the acquisition is to be paid for in yen or marks or some other foreign currency, then the foreign exchange risk involved in the transaction is readily apparent. If the acquisition is to be paid for in dollars, then the question arises, "What would the price be if we paid in local currency?" If the dollar is strengthening, a local currency price may mean a better deal for the buyer.

Companies that have extensive international sales have currency risk if they receive revenues in foreign currencies. These foreign currencies must usually be translated into the home currency, either because they are literally being brought home or because the company has to report them in home-currency terms on financial statements. The currency risk involved here may be transactional or economic. It is transactional if we are talking about the risk of a particular receivable gaining or losing value because of currency shifts. It is economic if we are talking about the effect of currency shifts on the business as a whole. For example, Monsanto has identified economic risk associated with its annual plan and budget process. Foreign operations are expected to return a certain level of foreign currency revenues during the year. However, these revenues are then translated into dollars for reporting purposes. Budget objectives are expressed in dollars, and when the budget is determined, it is determined using an assumed exchange rate. The foreign operations have an economic exposure. The actual exchange rate may change during the year. If it does, the results, the difference between costs and revenues expressed in dollar terms, will change also. This change is not related to a particular sales transaction but to the whole system of costs and revenues and how they will look under different economic exchange rate scenarios.

So companies that hope to identify their currency risk must carefully examine their competitive position and the way they do business. In large, complex companies, several different kinds of currency risk may confront various operating units. The exercise of currency risk identification should be carried out for each unit. It may be that some units have no competitive risk, while other units may. Some units may have extensive international operations and large transactional exposures. Others may be planning acquisitions or divestitures where currency risk management is in order.

What Is to Be Done

Natural Hedges and Operating Measures

Once the task force has identified risk, it is necessary to decide how best to manage it. The first step should be to address all operating measures that might help mitigate the effects of risk.

Currency risk is not always a bad thing. Companies that manufacture only in the United States and sell only in dollars did quite well during the 1985–1988 period of dollar weakness. When the dollar began to strengthen subsequently, some of these companies began to do less well. It is not currency risk, however, that caused them to do less well but ineffective management of risk. Currency changes are not an omnipotent, unmanageable, external force; their effects on a business are in every case manageable. A business manager who complains that currencies are unmanageable is like a sailor who complains that the wind is unmanageable; he merely testifies to his own incompetence. Managing sometimes means changing direction.

Managers ought to be able to take advantage of favorable currency moves while protecting themselves from unfavorable ones. Insofar as possible, companies should seek to pay their bills in weak currencies and collect on their receivables in strong currencies.

Purchasing

This means that companies should be able to shift costs when currency relationships change. During sustained, long-term periods of dollar weakness, it is best to rely on dollar-based suppliers. These may be located either in the United States or in other countries, such as Taiwan and Korea, whose currencies move generally in tandem with the dollar.

By the same token, during sustained, long-term periods of dollar strength, it is best to rely on suppliers located in countries whose currencies do not move with the dollar. Yen- or EMS-based suppliers are preferred.

For a company to maintain the flexibility of switching sourcing arrangements, it may be necessary to maintain more purchasing relationships than have historically been necessary. Purchasing staff ought to evaluate and approve suppliers, based in part on their ability to provide the opportunity of managing currency risk by shifting sourcing. This means that the approved vendor list should include vendors from different currency environments. Remember that a vendor whose currency is pegged to the dollar is in the same basic currency environment as a vendor in the United States. This becomes a particularly important consideration when long-term purchase contracts are at stake.

In fact, it is best to set purchasing contract price costs in local currencies wherever possible. If a supplier is paid in dollars, the supplier is forced to manage the risk of his own currency fluctuations with respect to the dollar. This means that when his currency weakens, he receives a windfall profit in local currency terms. On the other hand, when his currency strengthens, his margins are squeezed. The price that the supplier charges the company certainly contains a premium to compensate the supplier for the currency risk. It is preferable for the company to pay the supplier in local currency. This way, the company may retain the benefit of favorable currency moves and protect itself through unfavorable moves by various hedging strategies or by switching suppliers if the currency move is big and long-lasting.

Sales and Marketing

On the sales side, the company must seek to prevent currency shifts from decreasing its market share while also maximizing the advantage to be gained from currency moves that favor the company. One way to achieve this is to diversify into new markets that are not closely linked to the dollar and to bill in local currencies. During periods of dollar weakness, local currency revenues are worth more in dollar terms. The company retains the ability to cut local currency prices, but need not cut them if competitive circumstances do not demand it. A company that sets all of its prices in dollars automatically cuts its local currency prices when the dollar weakens. Actually, it is the currency markets that cut the local currency prices; they determine that although the product may cost the same in dollar terms, each dollar is worth less in local currency terms and therefore there has been a price cut in local currency terms. A company that wants to retain control over its pricing strategy ought to set prices in local currencies wherever possible and make price cuts or price increases part of a marketing plan rather than an incidental consequence of decisions made by bank currency traders whose collective manic depression sets relative currency values.

Hedging

There are two kinds of hedges: natural and financial.

A natural hedge matches the currency of revenue with the currency of cost. For example, manufacturing in the country where one sells creates a natural hedge. A company that pays its bills in the currency in which it collects on its invoices has a naturally hedged position. Costs and revenues move together, so margins remain constant.

Few companies are able to address currency risk solely through natural hedges. Economies of scale often make it impossible to put a plant in every currency environment where the company's product is sold. Raw materials, machinery and other production inputs, R&D, and other costs may not be susceptible to natural hedging.

Natural hedges are usually preferable to financial hedges because they are perfectly matched. Also, they provide protection without requiring the services of bankers or other vendors of currency risk management tools.

Yet when natural hedges cannot be put in place, financial hedges—forwards, options, and debts—ought to be used to manage currency risk.

A financial hedge moves inversely to whatever it hedges. In the case of a forward, for example, the forward position becomes more valuable as the currency it hedges becomes less so. Similarly, the forward becomes less valuable as the currency it hedges becomes more so. We have discussed at several points the experience of Lufthansa, which used forwards to hedge exposure to the dollar. Lufthansa entered into forward contracts, agreements to buy dollars at a fixed price, when the dollar was very strong—that is, very expensive—against the mark. Shortly after Lufthansa entered its contracts, the dollar became very weak—very inexpensive—in mark terms. Lufthansa's forward contracts lost value rapidly, a loss of roughly $140 million to $160 million, depending on the dollar-mark exchange rate used to translate the mark loss. That loss cost Lufthansa's senior financial management their jobs.

However, the loss was part of hedging. It is a very normal, natural thing for forward contracts to lose value as the currency position they hedge becomes more valuable. If, instead of weakening, the dollar had strengthened further, Lufthansa's forward contracts would have gained value, and management would have looked like heroes instead of scapegoats. Lufthansa's forward hedge looks bad with hindsight, yet it accomplished what it had been designed to do: It guaranteed that the price of a major purchase denominated in dollars would be fixed and predictable in terms of marks.

Lufthansa's forward hedge demonstrates one of the big disadvantages of forward contracts. Forward contracts are best used to hedge short-term exposures, ideally over a period of time unlikely to see extreme currency moves. A forward hedge can be very safe and very economical for a three-month exposure, but fatal when used to hedge a three-year exposure. The longer the time period, the greater the uncertainty. The greater the uncertainty, the greater the risk that the forward position will represent a wrong guess on the direction of rates. Forwards are firm and unforgiving. They can be unwound, but if the rates have moved against the hedger, unwinding the forward hedge will mean taking some losses.

It is in uncertain situations that options shine. Options have a known cost, a premium. Sometimes this premium is expensive. However, for hedging long-term exposures or uncertain sales forecasts, or for hedging any uncertain payment or receipt, options make excellent sense. The premium tends to be more expensive as uncertainty becomes greater. However, the premium provides certain knowledge of the cost of hedging the exposure. The hedger knows with certainty what the worst possible case is, and in fact has chosen and paid for it. Contrast an option with a forward. A forward provides no indication of what the worst case will be; it merely establishes a particular case as certain—whether it will be a good or a bad certainty does not enter into account. With an option, the hedger pays for choice.

Debt also provides a way to hedge currency exposures. A company with long-term revenue streams in a given currency can hedge that stream by borrowing in the currency. The borrowings act almost as a natural hedge because the cost of debt service will rise and fall just as the value of the revenue stream rises and falls. Generally, debt is used to hedge medium- and longer-term exposures such as long-term revenue streams and investments in subsidiaries.

Magnitude, uncertainty, and time are the three most important factors in arriving at a decision on what kind of financial hedge instrument to use. How large is the exposure? Small exposures may not be worth hedging. Very large exposures may require a combination of several hedge instruments. For example, when FMC experimented with a three-year hedge of forecast sales, it used forwards for one portion of the exposure and options for another. Forwards covered the part of the exposure that was certain to occur, and options covered the part that was less certain. Time usually means uncertainty. The future becomes less and less predictable the farther it gets from the present.

Organization and Controls

After companies have identified their exposures and familiarized themselves in a broad and general way with the characteristics of various hedging instruments, it becomes necessary to organize for currency risk management.

The first step here is to define clearly and unambiguously what the company's goals and policies are with respect to risk management. A policy must be agreed upon, set forth in detail, and clearly understood by all parties involved in the management of currency risk—in both the treasury and functional areas. The best approach is one that makes currency risk management the responsibility of the party who creates the risk in the first place. This does not mean that every purchasing agent who buys an imported part, or every sales representative who makes a foreign currency sale, must phone the bank to purchase an option, enter a forward, or incur debt to hedge the transaction. However, it does mean that these parties should be aware of the risk and act in accordance with corporate policy to address it.

Some companies, especially those that are very decentralized because they operate in many industries, make an effort to push hedging out into the field as far as possible. For example, at Monsanto, as at Allied Signal, treasury management has educated operating management to the instruments available for hedging, their possibilities, costs, and limitations. The decision whether to hedge or not to hedge, whether to hedge with an option or a forward or with debt, is made by operating management. Operating management then takes the consequences of its decision.

The benefit of making risk management the responsibility of the operating level is that currency risk is indeed an operating risk best managed in the context of other operating risks by those who understand them best: the operating managers.

In other cases, the company may prefer to remove currency risk management from the sphere of the operating managers. A company that approaches currency risk management as an opportunity to profit by trading currencies will prefer to concentrate all currency risk in one place so that it may be profitably managed.

Management of the Trading Function

Whichever approach is taken, the company must clearly spell out the policy, and the policy must be absolute. If the company intends to hedge all exposures, period, that intention must be stated in the policy and reinforced with appropriate controls. If the company intends to manage currencies in order to make money on them, that intent must similarly be spelled out. The statement of policy must address not only the objective but the means of reaching it, the level of risk that the company will tolerate, and the degree of autonomy, if any, that risk managers will have.

Currency trading is a verbal business, conducted for the most part over the telephone. A company receives a line from the bank and the company's trader can commit the company to the full extent of that line. For this reason, most companies centralize the trading function. Even when operating managers make their own decisions on how, when, and with what instrument risk may be managed, the actual execution of trades is usually done by one individual or a small group at headquarters.

Implementation of a currency trading function, whether the trading be for profit or for hedging, means establishing certain controls. The most important single control is the management policy. Within the policy, the most important point is the determination of whether the currency trader is expected to trade for profit or not.

Currency traders who make profits also make losses. A company that desires profits must also tolerate losses. Winning at foreign exchange trading means having more profitable trades than losing ones. It may mean having more profitable years than losing ones. Losing is part of winning. Nothing is more dangerous to a company's financial health than a currency trader who is afraid to unwind a losing trade because he fears that if he reports a small loss he will lose his job. Currency traders often take views, strong views, on which way the market is going. Professional pride may make it difficult for them to admit mistakes and bail out of losing positions. If, added to that, a company imposes a penalty for being wrong, all of the ingredients are in place for a major trading loss. Currency trading can be a profitable, long-term business in itself. However, any company that hopes to make money by trading must treat it as a business. That means investment in people, in systems, and in a learning curve. It also means that setting goals for traders is different from the way in which goals are set for salesmen. It may be reasonable to expect a sales force, building on last year's base, to increase revenues x percent in the following year, but it is not reasonable to expect that kind of performance from traders, especially if they must work with the raw material of a company's natural positions.

Currency trading, in other words, is not a lark. It is deadly serious business.

Whether a company enters the currency markets as a trader in search of profits or as a hedger looking to eliminate risk from certain business situations, someone in the company must be designated "the trader." The trader is the person whom the banks will know by telephone. The trader's voice is the company's voice. The trader's word is the company's word.

Certain controls are prudent. For example, the trader must never have the last word. That is, although he may commit the company to transactions, someone other than the trader must be aware of those transactions. Banks enter into trades with corporate traders, then, at the end of the day, call the company to confirm the trade. The confirmation call must never be taken by the trader who made the deal. The trader should have autonomy to make deals, but someone else should also know what deals have been made.

Banks usually double-confirm trades by sending a written confirmation. Many companies direct banks to send the written confirmation directly to the accounting office. The accountants usually work in a separate department from the currency traders, so this practice focuses yet another set of eyes on the transactions of the trader.

A clear policy and a good set of controls will minimize, if not eliminate, the possibility of losses from fraud or wild speculation.

Going Ahead

As long as floating currency rates are with us, currency risk will also be with us. In recent years, the inability of governments to provide stable currency relationships has become more and more clear. The Group of Seven (G-7) is an assembly of national economic chiefs who have agreed to cooperate in order to achieve stability of their currencies at levels that they think appropriate. In connection with this effort, the United States has promised to solve its budget deficits and Japan has promised to open its markets. Similar promises have been made by France, Germany, Canada, and Italy. It will require enormous political effort for each country to keep all of these promises. The status quo is a problem, but it would not be the status quo in the first place if it did not provide something of value to some powerful political constituency. Therefore, it is safe to say that solving the problems of the status quo by taking valuables away from the powerful may be a long drawn-out affair. Meanwhile, currency markets steer by their own lights, often moving in an opposite direction from the one G-7 prefers. The lesson for businessmen? Get used to instability and learn to manage it, because it will be around for a long while to come.

Currency risk affects every function of every business that uses money. It is part of purchasing, part of sales, part of finance, part of production. Companies that ignore currency risk, or who come close to ignoring it by leaving it to the green-eyeshade folks in a dusty corner of the treasury department, make a big mistake. Currency risk is a universal business risk, and must be managed in every function. Leaving all of the currency risk management decisions to an isolated group in treasury is like leaving all hiring, firing, and promotion decisions to an isolated group in the human resources department. What manager would let someone else pick his team? Why, then, let someone else pick his risks?

The developing awareness of currency risk is part and parcel of the global economy. As the boundaries between economies have grown more permeable, the old boundary lines between currencies have become less and less clear. Managing currency risk was not necessary when time, distance, and differences between populations made commerce rare and sporadic. But currency risk is now part and parcel of a world in which there are no American managers, no French managers, no Japanese managers, but merely global managers who happen to be in America, France, or Japan.

Probably between flights.

AFTERWORD

Exchange Rate Volatility and Currency Options

by Howard McLean

The post-1973 exchange rate volatility that Gregory Millman's detailed case studies document so clearly continues to make currency management difficult for financial managers today. Within a floating-rate-with-intervention scenario, exchange rates are continually on the move, making fools of forecasters as often as not.

This brief Afterword will hopefully be of assistance to financial risk managers in two regards: first, by illustrating a simple technique whereby a clear picture of the systematic nature of exchange rate volatility can be derived and studied as to its potential bottom-line

Howard McLean is Program Director of the Philadelphia-based Center for Currency Options, which provides intensive currency option risk-management training programs to corporations in the United States and abroad.

impact, and second, by providing a brief technical introduction to currency options.

Rate of Change

Exchange rate volatility is the fundamental determinant of currency risk. Exchange rate volatility is the rate at which currency values change. Consider Figures 1 through 3 showing the relative value of dollar versus pound sterling, wherein the $US-sterling rate of change, in other words the percent change between dates, is tabulated. Graphs illustrate the rate of change over four-, thirteen-, twenty-six-, and fifty-two-week time frames during the five-year period from 1984 to 1989.

Figure 1 shows the closing spot rate every Friday for the five-year period. Figure 2 shows the unsigned percent change for each Friday versus the rate four, thirteen, twenty-six, or fifty-two weeks earlier. Figure 3 rearranges these five-year sets of observations for each time frame, from smallest to largest, creating a cumulative distribution. Thus, reading from Figure 3, it can be determined that over a fifty-two-week time frame, the $US-sterling exchange rate varied by approximately 12 percent or more (vertical axis) 50 percent of the time (horizontal axis).

Basic cost accounting using these "odds" can be sobering. Consider, for instance, a product line marketed by a U.S.-dollar-based company in England. Assume a 12 percent before-tax profit margin and a twelve-month time frame. Over the five-year period documented by this study, such a company stood a fifty-fifty chance of an exchange rate movement equal to the entire profit margin. If the exchange rate move was favorable—that is, a sterling rise—the result was a doubled profit margin. If it was adverse—that is, a sterling fall—the result was a disappeared margin.

A "double-or-nothing" does not constitute comfortable odds for most product lines of most corporations most of the time.

(text continues on page 192)

Figure 1. U.S. dollar-sterling exchange rate, June 28, 1984, through June 30, 1989.

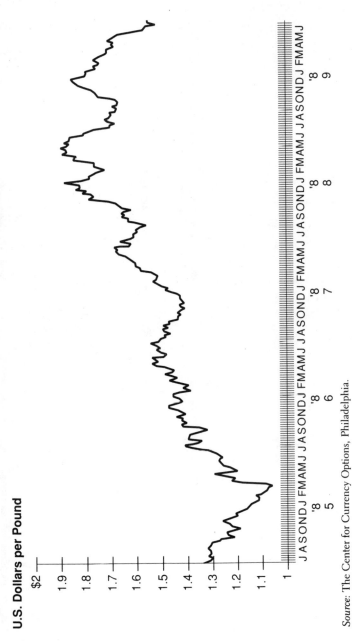

Source: The Center for Currency Options, Philadelphia.

Figure 2. Fifty-two-, twenty-six-, thirteen-, and four-week rates of change.

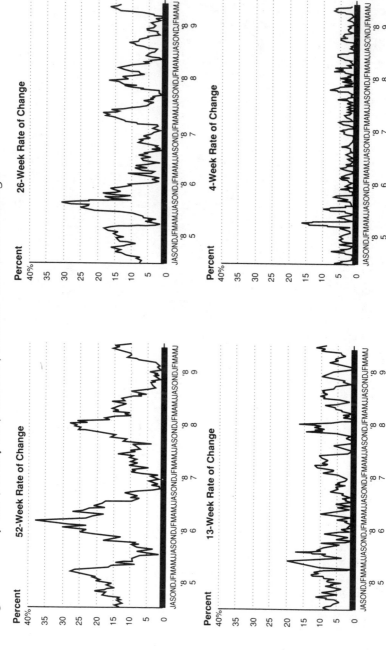

Source: The Center for Currency Options, Philadelphia.

Figure 3. Rate of change cumulative occurrence over five-year period, in percent.

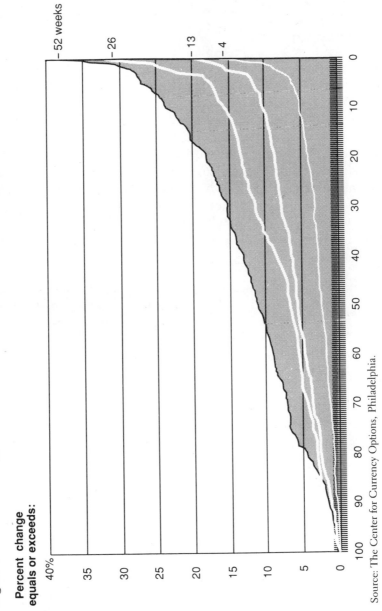

Source: The Center for Currency Options, Philadelphia.

Currency Options

Since the early 1980s, an entirely new financial market has emerged, grown in depth and diversity, and matured to the point of offering even the largest multinational a tremendously flexible set of tools for structuring and managing day-in, day-out exchange rate risk: the currency option market. In fact, currency options have become a primary alternative to the two time-honored approaches to addressing short- to medium-term currency risk: (1) the "do nothing" approach and (2) the forward hedge. The fundamental appeal of option-based strategies for managing risk can be understood when one considers alternatives. Refer to the $US-sterling rate of change from 1984 to 1989. Currency risk management alternatives include:

1. Do nothing, and, assuming the statistical volatility of sterling in the future will be in line with the recent past, accept the fifty-fifty chance that the rate will move by 12 percent or more against the underlying exposure.
2. Hedge in the forward market, locking in a known exchange rate for a specified date in the future—and also eliminating the possible benefit of currency exchange rates delivering a 12-percent-or-more increase in value of the underlying currency.
3. Use an option strategy that allows the hedger two advantages. First, the hedger can guarantee a worst-case exchange rate. Second, the hedger retains the benefit from a favorable exchange rate move.

The first choice, doing nothing, requires little discussion: If the hedger's convictions regarding the direction and extent of future exchange rate moves are strong and positive, he may make a case for doing nothing. Figure 4 shows the profit and loss potential of a £million exposure unhedged from a U.S.-dollar point of view. Result: open-ended possibilities in both directions.

The second choice, hedging in the forward market, is less straightforward. While the attractions of a known future rate are

Figure 4. Unprotected sterling position.

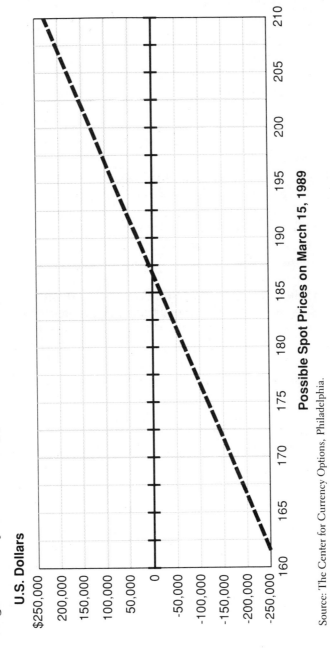

Source: The Center for Currency Options, Philadelphia.

obvious from an accounting point of view, the disadvantage is often less clearly perceived. The inability to profit from a future exchange rate improvement is somehow considered, all too frequently, to be of less than primary importance. For many corporations, forgoing profit potential isn't as bad as suffering a loss, especially if the company "is not in the foreign exchange business" and, by extension, shouldn't be looking to profit from exchange rate movements to begin with.

However, hanging the exchange rate outcome on one number, the forward rate, creates its own risk. Consider the situation vis-à-vis an *unhedged* corporate competitor: If the competitor reaps the benefits of a favorable exchange rate move, he winds up with a cost and pricing advantage. Thus, the corporation that chooses to fix an exchange using forwards may jeopardize its pricing structure and, ultimately, its market share. Figure 5 shows the net result of hedging with a forward contract: a locked-up rate that completely insulates the underlying position from movement in either direction.

Now consider currency options. Options give the upside advantage of doing nothing but retain the downside function of a forward. Figures 6 and 7 show two option-based scenarios, to be considered in turn.

Figure 6 illustrates the result of purchasing a British pound put option with a strike price of $1.85. By doing so, the put buyer has become entitled to sell £1 million at $1.85 any time up until a specified expiration date. (This is the case with American-style options. A European-style option can be exercised—only on the specified expiration date, but *sold* in the marketplace at any time.)

The key difference between purchasing options and covering in the forward market is qualitative: The option buyer has no obligation to sell sterling, only the right to do so. Clearly, if sterling is trading higher than $1.85 at expiration, he will forgo this right and sell at the higher spot market rate.

As Figure 6 shows, the put purchaser has a known worst case. If the strike price of the put is exactly equal to the spot rate value of sterling at the time the hedge is placed, the worst case outturn is simply the premium, or price paid for the put.

Figure 5. Protecting against a sterling decline with a forward sale.

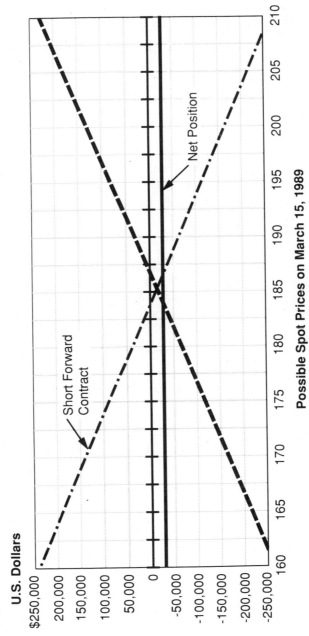

U.S. Dollars

Short Forward Contract

Net Position

Possible Spot Prices on March 15, 1989

Source: The Center for Currency Options, Philadelphia.

Figure 6. Protecting against a sterling decline with purchased put protection.

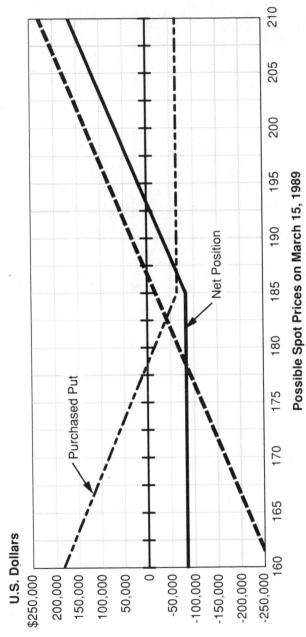

U.S. Dollars

Purchased Put

Net Position

Possible Spot Prices on March 15, 1989

Source: The Center for Currency Options, Philadelphia.

If the strike price and spot price differ, however, this difference also contributes to the worst-case outcome: a *lower* put strike price means both a lower premium and a gap between spot and the price at which the option protection commences. Since this gap is unprotected, it becomes the second component of the worst-case outcome.

On the other hand, if the put strike price is *higher* than the spot level, the put buyer will pay a correspondingly higher premium for the put *and* ensure a price level higher than current spot, which effectively improves his worst case.

The choice of strike prices for put protection illustrates another aspect of option flexibility, akin to purchasing insurance with a deductible feature. The higher the deductible, the lower the premium. Thus, a financial manager who feels strongly that the underlying currency will advance in value due to a favorable exchange rate trend can still place a (somewhat distant) floor beneath his position just in case he is wrong—and for a modest premium cost.

A second example of option-based hedging is shown in Figure 7, which depicts a strategy variously identified as a *range forward*, a *fence*, or a *cylinder*. Whatever its name, this strategy adds one more component to the simple put purchase of Figure 6.

A comparison of Figures 6 and 7 reveals that the most apparent difference is that in the former instance, the potential for benefiting from a rising British pound is unlimited, whereas in the latter case, a "lid" has been placed upon upside potential, at $1.95. The final result, then, is a known range for the final effective value of the sterling position, with a worst-case value of $1.85 or lower and a best case at $1.95 or higher.

The second, less obvious, difference between these two hedges is that while the worst-case loss still occurs at spot prices of $1.85 and lower, the size of that loss has been reduced substantially. In addition, the break-even (where the net hedge result crosses zero on the vertical axis) occurs at a lower spot price; in fact, at every spot price lower than $1.95, results are superior to the put hedge shown in Figure 6.

Figure 7. Sterling position protected with "range forward" or "fence."

U.S. Dollars

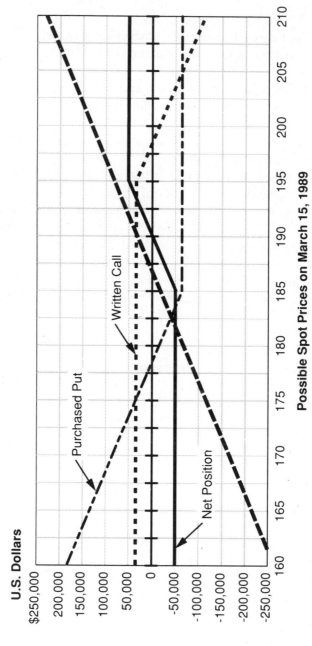

Possible Spot Prices on March 15, 1989

Source: The Center for Currency Options, Philadelphia.

The financial manager has accomplished this attractive final result by adding a second option component to his purchased put: a written call.

Option writers provide the option positions that are purchased by option buyers. In the put instance, since the put purchaser has purchased the right to sell sterling, the other party to the transaction must clearly have the obligation to buy the pounds in question if required to do so by the put buyer.

In the call writing instance depicted in Figure 7, the situation is reversed. Here, the risk manager is writing a call, which obliges him to sell sterling at $1.95 if requested to do so by the call buyer. In effect, by writing a call, the manager has agreed to share the upside potential for sterling; any improvement from the spot level up to $1.95 he retains, but he sells off the right to appreciation above that level to the call buyer.

There is only one reason to ever write an option: to earn the premium. In this instance, it is the earned call premium that substantially improves the hedge results over a wide range of potential spot prices. Since the writer intends to sell sterling in any event, writing a call in this context is not speculative, as it would be if no underlying pounds were actually on hand or anticipated.

This strategy, by whatever name, constitutes an attractive set of outcomes for a wide range of applications: on the one hand, the worst-case outcome is known from the onset, as with forward protection; on the other hand, a range of more favorable outcomes is also possible. This squares nicely with the need for protection and potential.

These two option-based approaches only begin to suggest the almost endless possibilities for structuring foreign exchange risk to meet the specific requirements of a given corporation at a particular point in time. A common comparison aptly suggests that using currency options successfully equates roughly to learning to play a credible game of chess. Both endeavors likewise imply a certain commitment to study and practice. Considering the stakes over which the exchange rate wars are fought, a growing number of companies have decided the necessary allocation of resources is clearly worthwhile.

Glossary

bid-offer spread The difference between the price at which a market maker will buy and/or the price at which it will sell a currency or a financial instrument.

call An option that gives the buyer the right to purchase currency at a specified price during a specified period or at a specified point in time.

covered call A call option written on a currency that the option writer either owns or will own.

currency swaps *See* **swaps.**

currency hedge *See* **hedge.**

duopoly A market shared or dominated by two suppliers only.

EMS European Monetary System, a framework that defines the value of European currencies relative to each other.

exposure Whatever stands to gain or lose value or efficacy because of currency exchange rate shifts. Exposure is often used as a synonym for **risk.** Exposures may be divided into *accounting* and *economic* exposures.

    Accounting exposure refers to the susceptibility of reported financial results to exchange rate moves. It includes *equity exposure,* the fluctuation in reported home-currency value of foreign equity investments, as well as *income exposure,* the fluctuation in reported dollar value of foreign currency earnings.

    Economic exposure refers to the company's ability to prosper in volatile exchange rate environments, and may or may not appear on reported financial statements. Economic exposures may be *competitive* if the effect of currency shifts will be to diminish or enhance a company's ability to compete. Economic exposures may also be *strategic exposures* in cases where the volatility of currency rates will help or hinder achievement of strategic objectives.

FX Foreign exchange.

FASB   Financial Accounting Standards Board.

forward   An agreement to exchange one currency for another at a future date, with the exchange rate fixed at the time of the agreement. Also *forward contract; forward agreement; to sell or buy forward.*

forward rate   The market exchange rate at which a forward sale or purchase may be made.

group of seven (G-7)   Seven major industrialized countries that have agreed to cooperate in an effort to stabilize exchange rates for their currencies. G-7 includes Canada, France, Germany, Great Britain, Italy, Japan, and the United States of America.

hedge   An asset, a liability, or a financial commitment whose value moves inversely to that of the underlying exposure so that the decrease in value of the underlying exposure is compensated for by the increase in value of the hedge.

naked   Uncovered; unprotected. An exposure left unhedged is said to be naked. Similarly, a naked call is a call option written by one who does not own the underlying currency.

natural hedge   A hedge that matches the currency of operating costs and operating revenues. For example, a company that pays manufacturing costs in the same currency it receives from sales is naturally hedged: A decrease in the dollar values of revenues is matched by a decrease in the dollar value of expenses so that margins are maintained.

netting   A currency management technique that offsets same-currency assets and liabilities against each other, then defines exposure as the net difference, sometimes called *netting value* or *net value.*

netting center   Usually a corporate office or subsidiary whose function is to perform the netting function by consolidating and offsetting currency cash flows among corporate subsidiaries, divisions, or operating units.

opportunity cost   The value that one gives up by choosing one course of action and excluding others. The value of opportunities forgone is the opportunity cost.

options   Agreements that give the buyer the right to purchase (in the case of a call) or sell (in the case of a put) a particular currency at a set price during a period or at a point in time yet do not obligate the buyer in any way. Options obligate the seller to act only when and if the buyer chooses to command.

premium   The price of an option.

put   An option that gives the buyer the right to sell a particular currency at a specified strike price during a period or at a point in time.

risk   Uncertainty that asset values, cash flows, or business objectives may be achieved or maintained. For example, *competitive risk* is the uncertainty brought to the competitive position of the company by currency moves. *Strategic risk* is the uncertainty of achieving strategic objectives because of interference from volatile currency values. *Hidden risk* may not easily be discerned by examining financial statements. Identifying hidden risk takes a serious analytical effort.

spot (also **spot market;** **spot rate**)   An exchange made "on the spot"— that is, immediately. Also, the price paid in spot transactions. Distinguished from **forward rate.**

strong   Valuable, expensive.

swap   An agreement in which two parties commit themselves to exchange a payment or a stream of payments in different currencies or different interest rates over a specified period of time. (In a *fixed-fixed swap*, for example, payments are determined by applying fixed interest rates to some notional principal amount. In a *fixed-floating swap*, one party applies an agreed fixed interest rate to the notional principal amount and the other applies an agreed floating rate to the same amount.)

transaction   A purchase or a sale. *Transaction risk* is the uncertainty of home-currency value of the expenditure or the revenue stream, and derives from a mismatch between the currency in which costs are incurred and the currency in which revenues are collected.

translation   The process of reporting in home currency terms the value of foreign currency assets and liabilities, usually belonging to a foreign subsidiary. *Translation exposure* comes from the risk that home currency values may rise or fall on the basis of exchange rate shifts between the home currency and the foreign currency, even if there has been no change in the performance of the foreign subsidiary considered in terms of its own currency environment.

unwind   To dismantle a financial commitment, generally by buying one's way out of it.

write   To sell, as in *write an option.*

Index